Giraffes of Technology

The Making of the Twenty-First-Century Leader

By

Dr. Hubert Glover, John Curry

ISBN-10: 1479349224
EAN-13: 9781479349227

Library of Congress Control Number: 2012917720
CreateSpace, North Charleston, SC

Foreword

by Dr. Bill Cosby

This is the most perfect foreword I've ever written, one that's given me great pleasure to tell. Please note that Mr. Glover (my Scout leader) and Dr. Hubert Glover are not related, but they mirror each other's leadership as revealed through the following story.

It was 1949 in north Philadelphia. My family lived in a housing project called the Richard Allen Homes, a community of lower-income families who were helped with subsidized rent to give them a chance to move in, move up, and move out to achieve better lives. The men worked, but their low pay prevented them from affording better housing. They had wives and children to support, and although the families weren't on welfare, most were poor and broke. My family lived in Apartment A at 919 Parrish Place, and above us lived a family (with three daughters) whose last name was Glover.

The girls' father, Mr. Glover, asked for and was granted a charter by the Boy Scouts of America to form a troop for the boys living in our section at Richard Allen. The Scouts waived the rule that we had to wear full uniforms, knowing that we couldn't afford them. Our mothers bought various parts of the uniform that they could afford, such as brown socks or shorts or the classic brown shirt. Some purchased the Scout belt. My mother bought me the neckerchief, but she couldn't afford the Scout slide, so my father taught me the Navy square knot to secure it around my neck. When Bobby Stevenson's father hit his lottery number—winning six hundred dollars—he bought a full uniform for Bobby, who immediately became our troop's flag bearer.

Soon Mr. Glover arranged for us to ride the trolley car out to Fairmount Park to march around in nature. There were thirteen or fourteen kids who (other than Bobby Stevenson) couldn't afford to wear the full uniform, but we wore enough parts that together we made up an entire uniform. It was our first time out in the park, where Mr. Glover taught us to identify plants and leaves. I touched a sassafras leaf and learned how to make the plant's tea. After we returned from the trip, I discovered that sassafras grew right outside of the Richard Allen projects, and I yanked up the plant, washed it, and made sassafras tea for my mother.

When we went camping, Mr. Glover taught us to start a fire using just flint and wick (to our amazement). Sometimes a few boys used Ohio matches with white tips, but when Mr. Glover caught them, he was disappointed and took the matches away. One boy threw a can of pork and beans into the fire, and it exploded. Police on horses came, and Mr. Glover apologized. The white police officer said it was quite all right. He saw our Scout leader as a man of nature and respectfully asked us to clean up the debris from the exploded can when we left so that the earth could heal again.

While we were cooking, Mr. Glover talked about helping people. I listened to his advice, and when I was back in the city, I'd tie on my neckerchief and go outside to help the elderly cross the street.

Many would get offended and say, "How old do you think I am?"

When I'd say that I thought I was helping, they'd respond, "Keep quiet, boy."

Even though my early attempts to help others failed, I continued to learn from Mr. Glover about the importance of giving to others. Years later, in 1971, when I played Chet Kincaid on *The Bill Cosby Show*, I devoted an entire episode to a character based on my Scout leader.

Mr. Glover gave. Mr. Glover resonated in my life and the lives of many others.

And that's the story of Mr. Glover.

I cannot think of a better way to acknowledge Dr. Glover's approval of my work than by telling him the story of Mr. Glover's leadership, which gave so much to the kids who lived at the Richard Allen Homes in north Philadelphia, and that somehow there is a strong Glover connection.

As an actor, educator, and business leader, I found that Dr. Glover's book captures the importance of ongoing learning while sharing knowledge and connecting with others, something we all should aspire to in our communities, and reflects how we should guide organizations through the twenty-first century.

* * *

Introduction

Reading, the Divine Gift

My maternal grandmother, Mrs. Mary Jane Smith, was born in 1876 in Camden, South Carolina, and her mother (my great-grandmother) was an American slave.

My grandmother never learned to read, and I suspect the same of my great-grandmother. Most slaves were not permitted to read or to practice any form of religion, which led to clandestine movements of reading combined with worship. Interviews, as well as transcripts of conversations with actual slaves, taken by historians suggest that worship served as a mechanism for survival. Reading gave slaves the ability to study the Bible, which offered ongoing learning and hope in the midst of despair.

Born and raised in Elmira, New York, my education was markedly different from my grandmother's. By age three I had learned to read at the All Saints Home Church of God in Christ, an African-American church founded in Memphis in 1907. Reading was a symbol of the highest achievement, offering the reader dignity and recognition. It was vital that a parishioner read before the congregation with the artistry of a skilled orator.

My parents were active, visible members of the church, so I felt added pressure to perform as eloquently as the adults. I practiced often because my parents required me to read aloud at home. The better you read, the more you were asked to read at church, a source of attention I embraced as a child.

Often my classmates and I left our Bible-study room in the church basement and climbed the stairs to the sanctuary, where we were asked, in turn, to read scripture before the congregation, an audience that could swell to more than two hundred. After my reading, I'd hear the applause and spot my parents' smiles. My ability to read and speak well at a young age grabbed the attention of my public school teachers. They appreciated my zest for learning and sought to reinforce it by giving me more to read, especially children's biographies of famous figures in US history, such as Mary McLeod Bethune, Harriet Tubman, and Frederick Douglass. I was intrigued by these leaders, especially educator and inventor George Washington Carver and President Abraham Lincoln, who both had gone from humble beginnings to great achievements because they spent much of their lives thinking about how to help others.

Teachers challenged me to tackle extra vocabulary and spelling quizzes, which increased my reading comprehension. Because I read well, I tested at a high level, a fact that in the early 1960s could determine your educational destiny. It was even more critical for black students to read well, or they would be placed in special education classes with children who had genuine learning disabilities. Often these misplaced black children became disenchanted by the time they reached junior high, reading at the first- or second-grade level, on course to become early dropouts.

Learning to read early led to my lifelong thirst for knowledge. Each day I searched for new information in class, at the library, or inside the bookmobile that roamed our neighborhoods. My companion was knowledge; my Internet was reading books. I traveled the globe through my eyes on the page. Because of my church—in effect my nursery school or Head Start class—by the time I completed the ninth grade, I was taking honors classes and had finished geometry, advanced algebra, high school chemistry and biology, and many of the English requirements.

Not to the Swift...

The church not only engaged me on a decades-long educational journey but also taught me emotional lessons, ones I continue to observe to this day. One of my favorite Sunday school teachers, Mrs. Susan Ellison, suggested I should never worry about what I can't do today but rather do what God has planned for me tomorrow.

Mrs. Ellison watched as kids teased me about my poor athletic ability, lack of social skills, and husky physique. She was the first black female I'd met who had earned a college degree, and she recognized my intellectual talents.

One morning after my Sunday school class, while the other children scurried into the halls and dashed up the stairs, she shared a passage with me from Ecclesiastes 9:11.

> *I returned, and saw under the sun,*
> *that the race is not to the swift,*
> *nor the battle to the strong,*
> *neither yet bread to the wise,*
> *nor yet riches to men of understanding,*
> *nor yet favour to men of skill;*
> *but time and chance happeneth to them all.*

Mrs. Ellison helped me interpret the passage by stating the popular paraphrase that "the race is not given to the swift, nor the strong, but the one who endureth to the end." She was introducing me to a real-world complexity I'd not encountered in my third-grade curriculum.

"Working hard and having faith are only part of life's equation," she once told me. "Humans need patience and time to reflect to allow real success to occur."

I must have looked puzzled, because she asked, "You know about farming, right?"

I nodded, having visited farms during our school field trips and on summer vacations at my grandmother's home in South Carolina. I had watched people plant seeds, nurture the soil, await the plantings to grow, and then reap the harvest.

"Your life is like that seed growing, Hubert. One day you'll be ready to harvest your gifts."

Like most of my young peers, I had absolutely no patience. I was ready to go, now. I wanted to get somewhere exciting. I'd witnessed how the popular and attractive kids got attention and rewards without working, without waiting.

Mrs. Ellison's comparison gave me a simple framework to connect what I was learning in church with what I was learning at elementary school. Soon I understood the virtue of patience, which helped me to have more complex dreams, ones with structure and long-term horizons, like licking an ice cream cone only after finishing my chores or buying a bicycle with money I'd earned from delivering my paper route.

Patience became an effective tool that guided me through the K–12 childhood. Mrs. Ellison preached that you need to see the gold in the ore before it goes through the furnace. Great talent or ideas never will be discovered if they're dismissed rather than encouraged. Most great inventions are created through trial and error. Patience adds structure and enables learning and growth. Patience is the fuel to see dreams realized, and dreaming was a way to see tomorrow beyond the realities of today. Mrs. Ellison's gift became a way not only to survive but also to thrive through optimism about my American future.

At night, my parents watched over me to make sure I said my prayers and read my scripture. They guided our family using two familiar verses. Psalm 23 is the famous prayer by King David—important to Jews and Christians—that casts God in the role of protector and provider. It's a statement of David's faith and a proclamation of his reliance on God.

> *The Lord is my shepherd; I shall not want. 2 He maketh me to lie down in green pastures: he leadeth me beside the still waters. 3 He restoreth my soul: he leadeth me in the paths of righteousness for his name's sake.*

We also read the following classic eighteenth-century children's prayer.

Now I lay me down to sleep,
I pray the Lord my soul to keep;
If I should I die before I wake,
I pray the Lord my soul to take.

Prayer was an essential part of our household. It was performed in the morning, evening, and before each meal. It highlighted a recurring theme of being thankful to have the fruits of labor such as a home and food; it was a reiteration of a message of hope for tomorrow. My parents asked for the safety of our family and for their children to have what they needed. When someone was sick, they asked for healing during their evening prayers. The morning prayer was in essence giving thanks for being awakened and for the hope of a good day.

The physical way we prayed was also important. We bowed our heads and knelt humbly as though we were approaching God. The lowering gesture indicated that no matter who we were, young or old, whatever demographic, we were the same—on the same playing field.

The work ethic of the community also was embodied in our prayers; we never prayed for anything lavish such as more money to make life easier—just the basics: health, shelter, and strength to continue to fulfill our obligations. The community was made up of Southern black migrants like my parents, or immigrants from far away. Their meager and simple existence in our small town was paradise compared to where they were born, and they focused on modesty, humility, and hard work.

My father told us that when he was a child his daily lunch was cornbread with sugar on top and, if he were lucky, maple syrup. My mother shared similar stories of how her mother had to spread simple meals to feed eight children, while often not having enough food for dinner. I also heard similar stories from classmates whose parents had come from Poland or the Ukraine. While on this Earth, we would work hard without expecting any grandiose outcome of riches that would relieve us of our daily toil.

While our daily prayers were important, the church building itself also had symbolic value. Our early church was ragged, although the tired building was where blacks in my community could do anything they wished. It was a critical meeting place for learning and friendship, growth and success. It was so valued that the congregation took risks to improve it, such as when my mother led a brigade of women in a fundraising effort with the distant goal of building a new church. Every Friday through Sunday, the congregation's women cooked fish and chicken dinners in the up-stairs kitchen of the old church. Sometimes they also used the Do Drop Inn next door to barbecue. The dinners were a major source of fundraising because the women sold them to the local manufac-turing plants.

Soon the dinners were in high demand from people of all backgrounds because the meals weren't sold as "soul food" but rather meat and vegetables seasoned with a Southern influence. The churchwomen also baked cakes and pies, which provided des-serts for the dinners and increased the time and labor they gave to raise funds.

Through these activities, I witnessed tangible examples of what hard work combined with faith would yield. The women labored all day at strenuous domestic jobs, washing and cleaning homes, cooking meals, and serving as laborers in the foundry where they poured hot iron into molds to make fire hydrants or fire engines. Then, each weekend, they cheerfully volunteered to cook and sell dinners to the community.

Green Pastures—and other local pubs—became a rich source of new customers who would leave their watering holes to enjoy home-cooked meals. As a child, I helped serve customers, cut po-tatoes, and box meals for delivery or pickup, always in awe of the tireless commitment of these women.

One day an architect arrived at our house to show us a rendi-tion of what the new church would look like. This was the first time I had seen the building at the conception phase. It was a simple brick structure, modest by today's standards, with a steeple and two entrances. The pastor's office and dining hall were located on the first floor. The sanctuary would seat three hundred people at full capacity, and the building would have offices, a kitchen, and bathrooms in the basement. The purchase price was nearly one hundred thousand dollars—expensive in the 1960s. After years of selling chicken dinners at three to five dollars apiece, the church made a down payment of ten thousand dollars.

This fundraising effort dominated my life until I was eight years old. When the new church opened its doors in 1965, it became the talk of our town because other black churches often bought an old church from a white congregation that had outgrown the facility. Ours was the first black church in the city to design a building from scratch with a professional architect, and the first service was recorded by WENY, the local NBC affiliate, which showed scenes on its evening news.

I witnessed women as entrepreneurs—another example of patience that spurred creativity and led to concrete, long-term success. I was proud of the women of our church, including my mother, knowing most had completed a journey from the Deep South to Elmira, New York, laboring as domestics and eventually owning homes in better neighborhoods. Now they worshiped in a solid, all-brick church they'd helped to finance, design, and build.

Those Were the Days...

My hometown of Elmira was a typical Northern industrial community where a strong work ethic existed among residents. The city had low unemployment in the 1960s and a vibrant economy based on manufacturing, with companies such as General Electric, Westinghouse, American Bridge, and various specialty manufactures. Elmira was one of the Northern target cities where people from the South migrated to find higher-paying positions rather than the agriculture-based jobs provided in rural towns from South Carolina to Mississippi. The city was also a major destination for immigrants from Italy, Poland, and Ireland.

In our community, owning a home, taking care of your children, and being a responsible person were highly valued. The theme song "Those Were the Days" that introduced the popular 1970s television show *All in the Family* could have been Elmira's theme song when I was growing up.

Boy, the way Glen Miller played. Songs that made the Hit Parade.
Guys like us, we had it made. Those were the days.
Didn't need no welfare state. Everybody pulled his weight.
Gee, our old LaSalle ran great. Those were the days.

Elmira was a rust-belt town with a population of fifty thousand, built in a valley along the Chemung River, part of the Erie Canal that flowed from Buffalo through Elmira. The river and railroad provided access to the city, which fostered the growth of industry and cultivated a community value in which charity wasn't simply pity but rather a community act of compassion and sharing. Back then, "charity" was a positive word, implying that you cared and were concerned about outcomes—not just getting something done. Charity was basic. It was a tangible act of love that distinguished us from animals. Early on, I learned that charity is a vital characteristic of leadership. Whether you're a teacher or lawyer or a CEO, outcomes are driven by the timeless trait.

We faced the same complex issues as any other town of the era. There were challenges in terms of race relations, especially between whites and blacks. In 1957, when I was born, the town was essentially segregated. The Irish, Italian, and Polish often lived in separate neighborhoods. Blacks lived in one section of town, away from whites. Integration existed at work and in schools but not socially at places such as the church, neighborhood bar, or meeting spots sprinkled throughout the city.

In the fall of 1956, my father chose to move our family from The Bottom, a predominately black community behind the railroad tracks near the river, to the white neighborhood of Pigeon Point, named after the pigeons that clustered around Victorian homes in the northeast corridor of town. My mother was pregnant with me, her last child, so my father planned to rent a duplex in The Bottom and eventually buy a larger home, where later I was born and raised.

One of the short-term results of my father's prescient act was that during the first three years of my life our white neighbors resented our presence in the neighborhood. They were not shy about their expressions. Our car and house windows were repeatedly shattered; my brothers were often attacked while walking to school or playing in the yard; and our neighbors refused to speak to us. Yet, stubbornly, my father trusted that the area was a better place for his family to live. The larger homes had porches and spacious yards. The neighborhood had parks and better schools. Our block surrounded a pond where the community went fishing and ice skating.

In the late 1930s, my parents journeyed north after the Depression and before America joined in World War II. They were in their early twenties and had grown up in the rural South with the region's lingering Jim Crow laws of separate schools, parks, restaurants, and public bathrooms. They knew how to be humble, to be "seen but not heard" yet still thrive. In Elmira they went to work, instructing us to attend school and not to worry about how the neighbors treated us. For my parents, owning a home in a good neighborhood was a "dream deferred," and not being readily accepted by neighbors was worth the progress.

As a young child in our new neighborhood, I enjoyed living with my older brothers, Gilbert and Raymond, thirteen and eleven years my senior. I cherished them because they could drive a car and go to parties, and they had loads of friends.

Once when Gilbert was returning home from school, I spotted him stepping off the city bus. I leapt off our front porch and sprinted to greet him. As I ran across the road, a van struck me, knocking me to the asphalt.

My parents were at work, but Mrs. DeAngelou, our white neighbor, witnessed the accident and was the first to reach me. With my brother's help, she carried me to her car and rushed me to the emergency room at Saint Joseph Hospital. She called my parents while I was frightened and crying, and she gently held and comforted me until they arrived.

When my parents learned from the doctors that I would be fine, Mrs. DeAngelou pulled my mother aside and apologized for how our neighbors had treated us. She told my mother that when the van hit me, all she saw was a child in danger who needed to be rescued, and she reacted without consideration of my race.

The accident changed our relationship with our neighbors in Pigeon Point. Other women had seen me get hit, and even though they hadn't acted, they were moved. That ice was broken. Neighborly conversations began, and in time my brothers and I played with other children and eventually were invited to play inside their homes.

The neighborhood mothers played a key role in my family's assimilation. Their bond was responsible for taming the racist lion's ongoing attacks. The accident stimulated the push to help the fathers in the neighborhood see our humanity too. Mrs. DeAngelou knew I was human; she saw blood on my knees—just as she had seen on her own children.

Rising from the Elmira Curse

Like many small towns in the US, Elmira had a timeless curse. Most residents spent their lives yearning to leave and experience the broader, exciting world, but often obstacles such as money, acceptance to college, or the strong connection at the right time prevented the serendipity that would alter their lives. Although small towns can be supportive, they also can be restrictive. Many people stick around the area as if they're shackled.

But that wasn't the case for international fashion guru Tommy Hilfiger, who was raised in Elmira. Tommy had eight siblings, so most kids in our town went to school with one of the Hilfiger children. After Hurricane Agnes devastated downtown in 1972, Tommy was allowed to use one of his friend's father's shoe stores to sell jeans out of the basement, which became the first People's Place store. Tommy would travel to New York City in the Canal and Battery Street areas, where clothiers produced their fashion lines or where the imports initially were shipped and merchants sold outdated lines. Tommy bought jeans and sold them in Elmira for five or ten dollars a pair. While they were outdated for New York City, they were way ahead of the fashion trends in Elmira. Tommy grew the People's Place business into a ten store business, which was located throughout upstate New York.

Even though Tommy introduced Elmira to big-city fashion, he remained a local guy whom everyone knew. I studied the unfolding of Tommy from his selling bell-bottom jeans to the opening of a store chain to becoming an international fashion magnate. He went from being one kid in a family of nine children to a business owner controlling his destiny. People traveled from all around to shop at one of his various locations. I proudly wore a T-shirt with his logo of people holding hands, a unique 1970s design that promoted themes of community. Without depicting any colors or genders, the T-shirt revealed various shapes of people holding hands in a horizontal line, suggesting an early global awareness that was uniting people across the world, a "new herd" setting.

When Ernie Davis, the first black Heisman Trophy winner, died of leukemia in 1963, a year after signing with the Cleveland Browns, the city was devastated because their hometown hero had fallen, reinforcing the idea of the Elmira Curse. Davis is forever cast in the annals of sports history as the gridiron hero at Elmira Free Academy and the history maker at Syracuse University, but his early death meant that Elmira would not receive national recognition. Elmira had so many promising athletes who never got drafted by the pros, as well as musicians who never rose to the top of the *Billboard* charts.

Elmira needed a hero. Perhaps this was why residents clung to Mark Twain, even though he wasn't from the town but had married Sarah Langdon, who had been a resident. So, watching Tommy reach this level of success (prior to my high school graduation), gave me a tremendous boost. Unlike any other hero I could name, Tommy Hilfiger was a local guy who had made it. I knew him. I'd met him. I'd wandered through his stores. Tommy helped make my goal to be successful more realistic and achievable.

Tommy embodied the values of Elmira—believe in it, work hard as you go after it, and the dream (even an aspect of it) will happen one day. He also did something for me that was critical. I saw the pride he brought to our town by having successful stores launched in nearby places such as Ithaca, where Cornell University is located, or Corning, where the famous glass company, Corning Glass, was located and is now a leader in the manufacturing of fiber optics.

Tommy Hilfiger shattered the curse of Elmira so that residents finally felt respect. He paved the way for others to follow. Many of us unconsciously believed in the Curse, but after seeing Tommy's international rise, we felt more optimism, rooted in a concrete example of an average guy who had left town to live in the big city, expand his thinking, and interact with people in *new herds*—and we wished to add our names to that list.

Life-Long Learning—Moving Forward to Feed

From 1965 to 1968, Bill Cosby appeared on *I Spy* as the first African-American male to star in an American TV drama. It was rare to see black men on television, and when you did, they often portrayed construction workers, butlers, or bus drivers. In contrast, Cosby's character, Alexander Scott, was a Rhodes scholar and had a close and equal friendship with Robert Culp's white character. This was cutting-edge TV in the 1960s and made a dramatic impression on me.

Cosby preached about the importance of going to college and would himself earn a PhD. I related to Bill Cosby because he was visible, intelligent, and respected, all of which were important goals of mine. He was an engaging role model when I'd had so few growing up. I looked to his life as a source of how I should conduct myself. Cosby and I both came from blue-collar, Depression-era parents, so it isn't surprising that he also embraced the values of working hard and caring for others while having faith to pursue a goal.

On *The Bill Cosby Show*, which aired from 1969 to 1971, he played Chet Kincaid, a gym teacher in a Los Angeles high school. Kincaid often counseled his students, and his character was depicted as a young, cool, black single male who promoted education.

In an episode in which Chet Kincaid was counseling a student in trouble, he encouraged the young man to find his own path, which turned out to be photojournalism. Soon the young man joined the high school newspaper staff and pursued a career after attending college. In the episode, Cosby mentioned the University of Southern California (USC) as having one of the best cinema and journalism schools in the country.

That was all I had to hear—Bill Cosby had spoken. I listened and soon selected USC as my target. At the Elmira library, I researched USC and discovered that Cosby was correct about the school's journalism department, which offered majors in both print and broadcast journalism. While I had photography experience from working on class yearbooks, my passion was broadcast journalism from my volunteer work at our local station. So USC was where I applied, and it was the only place I applied. I hung my school selection on my idol, who had emphasized higher education and USC.

Since my early days of listening to Cosby's comedy albums and watching *I Spy*, I had wanted to meet the man. When my daughter, Chanel, graduated from Florida A&M in December 2003, I sat near him. Cosby's brother, Russell, was in Chanel's graduating class, and the commencement speaker was none other than Cosby himself. After his rousing address, Chanel graduated, and I watched her shake the hand of the future winner of the 2009 Mark Twain Prize for American Humor.

Atlanta 2000: The Discovery of the Giraffe

When I left Elmira in 1974 to attend USC, my main references for leadership were my principal, pastor, and father, but after college I began to run with new herds as I toured the world as an auditor and a management consultant. I experienced a variety of business cultures and staff, as well as operating and management styles, which led me to keep asking myself (without ever finding a neat and tidy answer), "What makes an organization not only survive but also thrive?"

In the year of the millennium, I moved to Atlanta to start a challenging position at the largest consulting firm in the world, PricewaterhouseCoopers (PwC). The global accounting firm hired me to lead one of their subsidiaries, where I would manage more than two hundred people throughout North America and

Europe. At age forty-three, I had more visibility and accountability than ever.

Atlanta was a different city than it had been in 1978, when I had lived there while completing my MBA. In 2000 it was the continuing center of the New South, a hotbed for business, and an Afro-centric city with a growing black middle and upper class. Four years earlier, the city had hosted the Summer Olympics.

One Sunday morning along Peachtree Street, I sat inside the Shark Bar Restaurant eating brunch, reflecting on the fact that it was a new century and that I had one of the most stimulating jobs of my career.

I stared out the window at the gray sky, stirred by the challenges of my new position. I envisioned my future here in Atlanta, the possibilities—briefly returning to Elmira to hear long-ago-told lessons from my parents and favorite teachers, aunts and uncles, who consistently suggested I could do nearly anything with hard work, patience, caring for others, and faith.

"You look pensive."

The voice I heard interrupted my comforting act of dreaming.

"Are you a poet?" the waitress asked, standing before me, noticing my scribbles on a pad of paper.

I shared that I'd recently begun to experiment with writing poetry to become more introspective, something studies reveal that the arts—particularly literature—can do for the overworked CEO.

She told me she was part of a young poets' group and invited me to attend one of the local cafés that featured spoken word performances, a warm environment where each night poets stood on the stage during an open session. I was amazed at the collection of poems I heard one evening from the young and old with different backgrounds, ethnicities, and nationalities. There were expressions of politics, social challenges, and romance—a few even comedic. The evening engaged me. Common in each artist was an obvious joy, the satisfaction of expressing intense feelings and sharing emotions with others through the written word.

Poetry is reflective and expressive, revealing a new world that for decades I'd ignored as if it were underground, a clandestine activity during war. Soon the Atlanta arts scene opened itself up to me. Each weekend I'd visit the city's historic High Museum and Fernbank Museum, as well as various holdings at historic black universities and colleges such as Clark Atlanta and Morehouse, which Dr. Martin Luther King, Jr., had attended. Each museum had a unique focus on African culture. In 2000, Atlanta had one of the largest populations of educated and professional African Americans in the country. The city offered weekend outings where I spent time learning about Africa and African-American history. I attended festivals and visited friends' homes that featured art from the African continent.

Soon a striking motif stood out—*Giraffa camelopardalis.*

The giraffe's image was everywhere, depicted in plates and paintings, masks and sculptures. I spotted them as souvenirs in art stores and flea markets. There were giraffe themes for blankets, spoons, and statues—even T-shirts. When I asked friends why they collected giraffes, the response was always that they were cute or a symbol of Africa.

Needing more specifics, I researched the exotic animal, learning that giraffes had been paraded through Rome in 46 BC, were eradicated from Egypt in 2600 BC, and once roamed through many parts of Europe and Asia, where fossil remains have been discovered. From classical antiquity, the giraffe's image was depicted on vases, rock carvings, ancient tombs, and even the handles of ivory combs.

Physically, the giraffe's frame is structured for the broadest vision. The unique herbivore epitomizes environmental scanning, relying on its height and vision to manage and see beyond its immediate surroundings. Giraffes serve as *lookout posts* for the *herd* and other mammals that graze in the wild. They roam in open areas, avoiding the jungle, where they can't see their main predator, the lion.

The tallest of all land-living species, giraffes range in height from fifteen to nineteen feet. As they graze, they stand tall, *moving forward*, walking with dignity, keenly aware of their surroundings. They rarely sleep; a typical rest period lasts about five minutes. Their Superman-like senses, coupled with their dominant height, serve as a natural surveillance system, a comprehensive set of sensory tools to protect the herd.

"Little gets by giraffes," writes Jane Steven in *International Wildlife*. "Their huge eyes, the size of golf balls…offer a 360-degree color view of the world. From their vantage point at the second-story-window level, they can spot a cheetah two miles away."

The sensitive hearing of giraffes enables them to detect the noises of predators approaching. Many research scientists believe giraffes' petal-shaped ears help them to communicate at decibels that humans, and their key predator, the lion, can't hear, offering giraffes an additional defense mechanism to warn herds and other herbivores that graze nearby. When giraffes sense that danger is approaching, they turn their necks in a manner that serves as a warning sign. The signal enables the herd to react and guards against looming threats, even dangerous weather conditions.

Jennifer Margulis writes in *Smithsonian* that these "statuesque animals" are also social and affectionate. When they aren't nibbling on moisture-rich foods such as acacia leaves, "they're weaving their necks in and out and rubbing up against each other—just constantly physical and touching each other. It's almost like they're doing some kind of intricate ballet."

While giraffes are not predators, they do defend and fight when necessary. Their weight ranges from 2,600 pounds to almost four thousand pounds, so if they kick a lion with a hoof, the thrust and impact can be lethal. Often giraffes elect to run, reaching speeds of more than thirty-five miles per hour in seconds, but they cannot sustain such speed for long periods, which is why they live in open country, where they use their height, vision, and other keen senses to reduce conflict and protect the herd.

Not only are other herbivores attracted to graze near the giraffe, but humans also find themselves drawn to this unique animal. *Out of Africa* author Isak Dinesen describes herds of giraffes as "giant speckled flowers, floating over the plains."

In the "Kisii community of southwestern Kenya," cites *National Geographic*, "giraffe sightings inspire great excitement…[and giraffes] are encouraged to remain within the village lands because the Kisii believe that their great height allows them to see approaching good and bad omens."

While I was living in Atlanta, giraffe-inspired art work, photographs, and ongoing research led me to think differently about leadership—especially at the start of the twenty-first century, a complicated setting due to dramatic increase in technology that continues to trigger uneasy change in all of our professions.

Giraffes of Technology: The Making of the Twenty-First-Century Leader is rooted in six herbivore-inspired leadership traits that CEOs and managers must embrace over the next decade. Today's technology triggers a business environment that requires adapting to untidy change. The six chapters in this book are rooted in unique themes of the metaphor of the giraffe.

- Acting as a *lookout post*—the ability to see further down the plains than most with a keen focus on long-term (rather than short-term) problems as well as opportunities.

- Communicating with others as *gentle giants*—a leadership style that engages rather than dispirits the herd.

- Dealing with *a violent birth,* the dramatic fall after which the infant giraffe struggles to rise, as a new business does.

- *Moving forward* to feed (engaging in ongoing learning)— the art of creating much more freedom in work settings to generate creative ideas that help employees adapt to ongoing, messy change.

- Understanding that the *lions of change* endlessly attack to maintain static work environments instead of embracing authentic change.

- Blending into *new herds,* a twenty-first-century environment in which diverse groups of people instinctively work together to deal with complex problems, thereby reducing last century's emotional work environments that inspired conflict.

CHAPTER 1

The Lookout Post—
Giraffes of Technology

From our car we could see giraffes, zebras, wildebeests, and hartebeests placidly feeding side by side. Suddenly, an enormous bull giraffe snorted in alarm and broke into a gallop. Every one of the animals bolted and followed. A few hundred yards distant, they all stopped to look back: three hungry lionesses had risen from cover close to the abandoned grazing site. Their game up, the big cats headed into the bush to look elsewhere for dinner.

—EMILY AND OLA D'AULAIRE, WILDLIFE WRITERS, 1974

Mary Jane Smith, my maternal grandmother, lived from 1876 to 1978. During her 102 years on Earth, she experienced the stable period of the agricultural and industrial ages. Near the end of her life, she was exposed to stirrings of the glittery information age. By living longer than her contemporaries, she learn to adapt to major shifts in technology as though they were nothing more than gaining a few pounds or spotting strands of gray hair.

My grandmother was raised in the Deep South, where she met and married my grandfather. The two moved around a great deal before landing in South Carolina. As a young wife, my grandmother learned that blacks needed to walk lightly in the 1930s Jim Crow setting. Decades later, though, she witnessed Martin Luther King, Jr., leading the cause for civil rights. Near the end of her 102 years, she witnessed the benefits her children and grandchildren reaped after the passage of the Civil Rights Act of 1964 and the Voting Rights Act of 1965.

Early in life, my grandmother had no electricity, just a pump and plow. She grew and canned her own food. Eventually she enjoyed the luxury of electricity, the radio and television, an automatic washer and dryer, and in-house toilets with city water, even though she still used a wood stove and made her own soap as late as the 1960s.

As with most Americans of her era, change came at a very slow pace; innovative technology was broken up by decades before a new product was introduced, mass produced, and accepted by the public. Because of these gradual shifts, my grandmother never became paralyzed by technology. She encouraged her kids and their neighborhood friends to experiment with her telephone and listen to her radio—the first one on the block—on Sunday evenings.

Change arrived in peaks followed by valleys, a slower setting that's been dramatically altered in the twenty-first century. My grandmother received a hint of today's hyper-connected environment during her last decade of life when she witnessed the first man to walk on the moon (1969); the first pay-TV network, HBO (1972); and the first home PC (1977).

She understood what was coming.

Giraffes of Technology

As I became enamored with the giraffe in Atlanta, I toyed with a unique comparison; in the natural world, giraffes have physical traits, habits, and social behavior that are comparable to those of leaders I'd admired in business, government, education, and sports. The most obvious trait was the giraffe's dramatic physique, which provides a sweeping vision across the plains of Africa. The giraffe's frame is structured for the broadest view. The tallest animal in the world epitomizes environmental scanning, relying on its height, vision, and alertness to manage and see beyond its surroundings—serving as a reliable lookout post for the herd.

The giraffe triggered a memory from the early 1990s when I was sitting in a packed crowd as MIT's futurist, Peter Senge, spoke about the need for learning environments—a cutting-edge theory he presented at conferences throughout the world. Senge stood out like the giraffe. His message was powerful, his ideas stimulating. He spoke about how to run companies in the second part of the information age, a highlight that stuck with me for years and led to my focus on the *giraffes of technology.*

More than any other time in US history, leaders now need to serve as sturdy lookout posts for herds. Senge urged businesses to embrace the value of—and the need for—learning organizations. His ideas parallel certain characteristics I find in today's social media where there are no strict boundaries, where information is freely shared, and where there is less fear of failure or being condemned for what you say or share. In its purity, the Web is a learning environment.

In 1999, Senge was named "Strategist of the Century" by the *Journal of Business Strategy.* He's the definition of a lookout post that continually scans the horizon. In 1990 he wrote *The Fifth Discipline,* a book that predicted that business was entering a time of quickening pace where there would no longer be a stable environment. Society would be bombarded with ongoing change and must be more alert through intensive, ongoing learning. Senge suggested that when encountering rapid change, only companies that were "flexible, adaptive, and productive" would excel.

He argued that companies must begin to see their employees as people, as assets to develop and feed through learning. The industrial-age terms "human resources" and "personnel" would shift to "human capital." To keep up with change, companies would need to become sincere learning organizations and decentralize the power of the old industrial-age hierarchy, bringing human characteristics such as the ability to adapt to a changing environment.

Senge viewed companies as organic entities that needed to adopt behavior that emulates learning. In *The Fifth Discipline,* he writes about "organizations where people continually expand their capacity to create the results they truly desire, where new and expansive patterns of thinking are nurtured, where collective aspiration is set free, and where people are continually learning to see the whole together."

Senge tapped into values from my Elmira upbringing, ones I hadn't fully connected to a business setting. Like the child who learns, adults also become energized. The educational act inspires passion, moving individuals beyond the industrial-age cliché of "Come to work early, work hard, and achieve."

More than ever, leaders and employees need an inviting setting in which people come early and stay late because the setting is one where they can be loyal to themselves and the company. CEOs must create inspiring environments of learning where everyone feels the freedom to take risks and fail, learn and succeed. A company sincerely designed to nurture and expand the number of lookout posts within its culture will have a vital mechanism to spot hidden opportunities as well as looming threats.

Early on, Jack Welch exemplified Senge's organizational model for companies committed to lifelong learning when he transformed GE after taking over as CEO. The company always had been well regarded by consumers, Wall Street, and employees as a leading organization. At the end of the nineteenth century, GE was ranked as one of the ten top-selling companies in the United States and was one of the original twelve companies that formed the Dow Jones Industrial Average. More than one hundred years later, GE remains among the top twenty-five global companies in terms of market value.

As reported in *The Jack Welch Lexicon of Leadership* by Jeffrey A. Krames, a year before Welch took the helm in 1980, GE was honored as the "Best Company in America" by Fortune 500 executives. Despite the company's success, Welch saw a need to transform GE from a century-old manufacturing company into a "learning culture in which ideas and intellect preside over tradition and hierarchy."

At GE, Welch created a learning process that strove to capture information and interpret its value for making the best strategic decisions that would position the company for continuous leadership in the marketplace. Employees were motivated and financially supported to come up with creative solutions to problems. The "informality" and "boundarylessness" at GE sparked the company's learning culture, which Welch defined in his speech at the 2001 Annual Shareowners Meeting as a "high-spirited, endlessly curious enterprise that roams the globe finding and nurturing the best people and cultivating in them an insatiable appetite to learn, to stretch, and to find that better idea, that better way every day."

Welch's unique style transformed GE from a pure manufacturing company to one of the world's largest financial institutions, supporting the backbone of several credit card, mortgage, and business-to-business operations while continuing to be a world leader in key products such as gas turbines, jet engines, and energy systems.

GE's learning culture led to the shedding of its well-known light-appliance business—which included the manufacturing of toasters and electric can openers—in the 1980s to focus on new industries such as providing capital to businesses. The company is still viewed as a market leader, the only remaining member of the original twelve members of the Dow Jones Industrial Average. The other eleven either have gone out of business or have been acquired by other firms.

Peter Senge and Jack Welch weren't alone in their ability to see further down the plains than most. Near the end of the '90s, two fresh *lookout posts* guided *herds* by communicating vital information, building on Senge's idea that "real learning gets to the heart of what it is to be human."

In 1998, Stanley Davis and Christopher Meyer published the book *Blur: The Speed of Change in the Connected Economy*, which examines the velocity of change in the emerging global environment. There's been a shortening duration of economies, they explain, beginning with the hunting-and-gathering period that lasted about one hundred thousand years before the transition to agrarian economies—a period of ten thousand years that was labor and land intensive.

During the transition to the industrial era (the 1760s to the 1950s), the emphasis shifted to machines and factories. And in the modern information age that began in the 1960s, supercomputers were used to crunch data.

At the beginning of the 1990s, however, we entered the second half of the information age, propelled first by the Internet and later by the Web 2.0. Davis and Meyer argue that from 1960 to 1990 not much had changed in terms of how we lived. We already had television and radio, cars and airplanes, and our living patterns were pretty much the same—static.

During the 1990s, however, the world began to change due to the exploding use of technology, spurred by business and government. The authors accurately predicted that the speed of change would be faster than it had been in prior decades, and companies and people needed to be prepared to anticipate change and respond in a timely and effective manner. The authors explain that we've moved into a time when there is no "clear line between structure and process, owning and using, knowing and learning, real and virtual.... On every front, opposites are blurring."

Many of us live in homes that are offices. We buy a product from a store, and later we sell it on Craigslist. More valuable than the data-crunching of the 1960s is the information, emotion, and connectivity of today that is, as Davis and Meyer explain, "people to people, machine to machine, product to service, network to network, organization to organization."

I became aware of this shift while managing the accounting department at Howard University. My business, Rede, Inc., grew by 327 percent from 2004 to 2007 and won an award for that growth from Texas A&M. There's no way I could have effectively managed the intense multitasking without technology that removed barriers of the past. Through the Web's speed of information and connectivity, I successfully managed my university classroom and Rede, Inc.'s administrative duties while devising strategies for the continued growth of my company. Today I can be an active CEO, professor, civic leader, and family man—something impossible in the past.

Kevin Kelly, executive editor of *Wired* magazine, is a recent giraffe of technology, who offers a positive view of the digital age with links to history, biology, and religion. In his 2007 TED lecture, Kelly cites that the Web is less than five thousand days old but has the processing power of the human brain. Through hits, clicks, and links, the Web mimics the brain's neurons and synapses.

Kelly raises an important question. Where will this single machine (one we enter daily through laptops, cell phones, iPads, and servers) be in another five thousand days? Technology is like human evolution or the Big Bang that expanded our once-compressed universe, causing growth and diversity. Beginning with the hammer, technology continues to expand our culture, which Kelley defines as "an accumulation of *ideas*."

Kelly envisions that over the next five thousand days there will be more connections and an abundance of never-ending breakthroughs "rolling into our lives." Kelly's giraffe-inspired predictions are that the Web, this singular global machine that we connect through, will only become more complex. Today the Web offers more fifty-five trillion links and receives more than one hundred billion clicks per day. More than two million email and one million instant messages are sent every second. Kelly predicts that in the next thirty years, the Web will exceed the processing power of all humanity.

In the new world of the Web, with this "black hole sucking up everything," making everything connected, what will the new economy look like? Kelly sees a future economy that will be based on a hybrid of the atomic and the digital. Every "noun" in the material world eventually will have an "embedded digital [intelligence]: cars, electronics, dogs, cats, children, picture frames, you name it. It will be a mix of the old (industrial) and new (informational or digital)."

As humans in the twenty-first century, we will link not just from machine to machine or webpage to webpage but also from data to data. Much of this data will be about us and spur relationships. Kelly cautions that we shouldn't be afraid of the Internet but should understand the twenty-first-century motto "To share is to gain."

Kelly envisions the Web as a single machine that connects us all through a new democracy that has nothing to do with majority rule; rather, it will be a tool that sophisticated societies will use to short-circuit lengthy and wasteful arguments. The Web, Kelly says, is "more powerful than we thought. It is more extensive, it's more humanizing, and every step of the way we are showing again how wrong George Orwell was."

A Brief History of the Lookout Post

Is the US going the way of Sears?

Most of us came of age hearing or reading Aesop's fable "The Tortoise and the Hare," about the infamous race between the over-confident hare and the humble tortoise. In the midst of the competition, the swift hare chose to nap—so sure of victory—only to awake to the news that the slow but patient tortoise had won the race.

Americans over forty recall Sears as though it were a dear yet deceased family member. Sears used technology of the late 1800s to become the hare of its day. It wisely used mail-order catalogs to bring the retail store experience into the homes of rural America that city stores were unable to serve. Through the smart use of nineteenth-century technology and the latest delivery methods (railroads, parcel post, free delivery, and the printing press), Sears became the fabric of American capitalism.

But by the middle of the century, an Arkansas tortoise had entered the race. Walmart was listening to small-town rural America and realized that these remote areas needed retail stores. Walmart spotted a need, and over the next sixty years, it leveraged technology to become the largest company in the world. Walmart used barcodes to manage inventory and minimize investment while maximizing its buying power to secure the lowest price. Technology enabled Walmart to predict buying behavior, observe trends, negotiate to meet current needs, and anticipate new demands from consumers so that products wouldn't sit on shelves.

In late 2007 through 2008, the effects of the Great Recession shifted customer needs from frills (electronics) to basics (toilet paper, toothpaste, and water). While most businesses were struggling in retail, Walmart's sales figures continued to rise because the company could anticipate the sudden shift in buying patterns.

At one time, Sears was a leading giraffe of technology with novel use of mail-order catalogs, the cutting-edge technology of the day. Over the decades, however, Sears had the luxury of being on top and no longer felt the pressure to serve as a lookout post. The retailer failed to discover the latest innovative products or access information to predict new trends and monitor the desires of their customers.

The key goal in creating Walmart was to fill specific needs of communities that weren't being served well in the early 1960s. Walmart told these communities, "Hey, you're more important than this."

So Walmart acted while Sears napped. Walmart abandoned the use of the paperboard box for deodorant in the early 1990s because it wasted cardboard and reduced space on shelves. Eliminating the box rescued forests, saved money (five cents per box), and cut fuel cost in shipping. Walmart, the consumer, and the nation saved hundreds of millions of dollars after the box vanished. The company soon became a *giraffe of efficiency* through green practices and consumer purchasing power.

Walmart also embraced a dynamic cradle-to-grave relationship with its suppliers. It shifted from "just ordering" to asking suppliers to join its team. Walmart sells nearly fifteen percent of Procter and Gamble's products, such as Crest toothpaste, so P&G's collaboration with Walmart in a herd-inspired partnership made sense.

Walmart said to suppliers, "You are as important as I am to you. I'm committed to having the lowest price for the customer, and together we're going to do well." With a commitment from Walmart, suppliers such as P&G could plan and manage production schedules and supplies. They also shared ideas regarding product design, packaging, and marketing. Everyone was working with a shared focus to keep prices low.

Walmart never feared innovative technology; rather it embraced it. Products such as Supply Chain Management (SCM), Electronic Data Interchange (EDI), and Just in Time (JIT) emerged with the capability of real-time ordering. Walmart was able to respond to purchasing trends and offer low prices.

Because of access to new technologies, Walmart knew exactly when it needed more detergent in Fargo, North Dakota, or more carrots in Buffalo, New York. Sears and other retailers never made these investments as early or extensively as Walmart, which used them as the core of its lookout-post operational strategy. Sears was never serious about the competition of Walmart, Kmart, or anyone else in retail. The Sears collapse began with the shift of Americans from rural towns to the city and the increased use of the automobile, which destroyed the retailer's decades-old mail-order business model.

Sears failed to focus on the long-term view that the US middle-class wouldn't expand indefinitely. As the leader in middle-brand products for middle-class families, Sears believed their success would continue. In 1973, however, US demographics shifted. The growing upper middle class began to shop at Bloomingdale's and Macy's while the growing working class—whose incomes were static and jobs less secure—searched for cheaper goods at retail stores such as Walmart. Sears felt its historical dominance was enough to carry the company along and failed to translate their success to new generations.

Sears was once the American flag swaying inside the nation's household, dominating the US retail market. But the company couldn't stir from its midrace nap as Walmart crossed the finish line and prepared to enter a new race in the hyper-connected twenty-first century.

The Danger of Flying Too Close to the Sun

In the timeless Greek myth of Icarus, the inventor Daedalus (the father of Icarus) created wings so that he and his son could fly from the island of Crete to their home in Athens. During the trip, Icarus chose to fly near the sun, leaving his father beneath him. The wax that held his wings together melted, and Icarus plummeted to a death at sea. The myth triggers themes of the danger of hubris and testing limits and boundaries, and cautions how we all have an overambitious youth trapped inside us seeking to soar.

In 1962, Anne Sexton updated the Icarus myth in her poem "To a Friend Whose Work Has Come to Triumph." In a modern-day twist, Sexton doesn't condemn Icarus for flying near the sun, which prompts his fall; instead she writes, "Think of that first flawless moment over the lawn" and "Admire his wings!" and "Who cares that he fell back into the sea?" Sexton finds positives in overcoming challenges and the excitement of attempting to achieve something extraordinary, even if one fails.

The poem has an original and accurate take on modern leadership, and Sexton's slant is vital when combined with Daedalus's long-term goal to land in Athens rather than the short-term crash into the sea. Today, however, there's compelling evidence that most companies act more like the adolescent Icarus by taking dangerous short-term risks. Leadership is best when ideas and risks are sustainable and implemented, guiding the overambitious youth (the hubris within us all) through learning settings, which can reduce Icarus-like plunges.

Sears is not alone in its sixty-year fall to the sea. Toyota's CEO, Akio Toyoda, testified before Congress in 2010, stating that his company had let go of its core principles. Toyota was once a symbol of quality that focused on the consumer's pocketbook, seeking to provide a low-maintenance and durable car that retained its value over time by remaining on the road. For decades, Toyota had avoided the short-term focus on dramatic growth, profits, or gains in market share and followed a more progressive model that led to industry domination, making it the largest car manufacturer in the world.

Toyota promoted teamwork among its employees with daily chants. The company invited and encouraged employee input on improving the craft of production, especially if it added value to the customer. But as the company grew, it shifted its focus to market share and profitability and away from the consumer, which led to its modern production problems and a recall of more than eight million cars and the temporary suspension of several models from the market. The company once known for quality was now battling a legion of class-action suits over poor craftsmanship.

In the *New York Times* editorial "Adults Only, Please," Thomas Friedman highlights Dov Seidman, the CEO of LRN, who discusses *situational* (short-term) versus *sustainable* (long-term) values. Seidman is right in his assertion that we're living in a situational era, one in which short-term thinking ("Do what you want without regard for the future") wins time and again.

Before its massive growth, Toyota was keenly focused on the quality of its products and customer needs. In a rush to expand, however, it shifted focus from its core values of fixing dangerous software problems (which require long-term thinking) to making short-term repairs.

Hubris often leads to taking short-term risks, which distracts an organization's core ideals and sustainable vision. Growing fast just for the sake of revenue is akin to young Icarus flying above his sensible father and too near the blazing sun. Smart companies should fly above Daddy but below the sun. They should focus on taking wise risks that have potential to last.

In the 1980s, when management literature was looking at Japan, many authors mentioned that Americans were obsessively focused on market share. But the Japanese zeroed in on providing the best cars to customers while continuing to be innovative. Toyota's result was increased market share, while the US auto industry plunged to the sea for decades. Toyota earned its market share by providing reliable, inexpensive, and outstanding automobiles that honestly reflected the company's brand and core values.

Toyota's model dramatically changed in the 1990s when it started to build cars outside of its home country of Japan and moved into China, Malaysia, the US, and other countries to meet global demand. The company failed to ensure that these new plants used Toyota's well-established lookout-post principles.

Short-term, *situational* focus on market share keeps popping up here in the United States and around the globe. Look at the headlines over the past ten years. The strategy is in vogue, and it's destructive. This short-term addiction seriously affected Toyota, once the most reliable car company on the planet. Fifteen years ago, could anyone imagine that Toyota's CEO would be on The Hill testifying for two days before the Congress of the United States?

That's the inevitable outcome if companies act solely through Icarus-inspired hubris.

Twenty-First Century Lookout Posts— Google and Buffett

Many companies today are adopting the "servant," "progressive," or "ethical" leadership model because it's in style. For most companies, however, it's a façade, a public persona, the face they keep in a jar by the door.

Like Sears, most companies are clinging to the archaic industrial-age model of leading companies. This isn't the *lookout-post* style vital in our increasingly transparent era via the Internet. Many leaders continue to define success as earning enormous short-term profits for companies and shareholders, despite the lingering effects of the 2008 Great Recession.

But hasn't this been going on for millennia? Yes, of course. Ego, money, and short-term decisions are timeless. But this "me" attitude, a ubiquitous leadership style, is a twenty-first-century trap. Over the last decade, it has intensified and negatively affected our economy, educational system, energy policy, and national infrastructure, and the list goes on.

Americans must wake up and ask more from companies as we speed through the twenty-first century. We need to adopt a sincere (not veneer) value system that's deeply engrained in an organization's DNA, one that inspires a view further down the plains and produces innovative ideas that benefit broader herds.

Leaders need to inspire another World War II generation, one in which the majority unites to solve increasingly complex global problems because they desire to act, because they were raised and educated to do so, and because it's about you—and me.

The giraffes of technology warned that the world economy is shifting at a speed that was once an absurd plot in a 1950s science fiction novel. Not today, America; if we don't respond to lookout-post warnings and opportunities, we won't excel in the global economy where the developing world meets the post-industrial developed world and "we" (not "me") attempt to solve serious global challenges.

There's hope, though.

The US once embraced the united approach, and each day lookout posts are born and raised to serve new herds.

The Rise of Google, the Postmodern Lookout Post

Google was created to help ordinary people navigate a new frontier called the Internet. Sergey Brin and Larry Page had no clue how to make money. Ironically, that's precisely why Google became the most lucrative search engine on the planet. Two geeky grad students attending Stanford dreamed of building a better search engine to serve others.

It was that simple.

Ten years ago, Google envisioned that the Internet was wonderful but would become dysfunctional unless they helped harness the virtual beast. They wanted to make it accessible and useable to all—a virtual democracy. Today you don't need a PhD in engineering to figure it out. Google embraced Kevin Kelly's prediction of how big the Internet would become through artificial intelligence that will develop the Web faster than the human brain can process information. Other tech companies were myopic, focusing on creating a browser, router, or cell phone—those necessary devices and sparkling gadgets. But Google's focus was to create a free and open software system that offered information to people as quickly as possible.

Brin and Page were curious, fearless, and humane. They excelled during the tech bubble-and-burst while most dot-com companies plunged. Engrained in Google's DNA was a genuine value system of helping others. Off-the-chart intellectually, Brin and Page also were mature emotionally. Gifted critical and creative thinkers, they enjoyed intense yet respectful debate. And they were obsessed about creating a first-rate search engine to explore a virtual galaxy.

Google's Customer-Centric Advertising

Eager to act as a lookout post, Google shattered traditional leadership rules. Central to its innovative technology was a concern for how the search engine would affect users—including Google advertising, which employs a less-invasive ad model that won't shut down computers. Brin and Page selected a front page that was minimalistic and pure. Search results load quickly because they eliminated flashy multimedia ads, a lookout-post choice that left out plenty of short-term money that was up for grabs.

They wanted users to receive the highest-quality search results that could improve their lives. Today, Google advertising makes gobs of money, but that was secondary. Brin and Page are tech artists who envisioned their search engine as a masterwork. Students and colleagues often ask me if you can seriously sell products and earn good money while primarily looking out for costumers.

Yes, I tell them. It is possible and difficult. It's a 2012 challenge that's the smartest long-term or sustainable path forward for customers, employees, companies, and shareholders.

Google's Values Guide a Long-Term Vision

Values are in Google's DNA and influence long-term action. Values are vital to lookout-post ideas because they restrain weak decision-making due to pressure, emotion, and stress. Values allow for more collaboration and learning, which reduces top-down, snappy decisions. To have a genuine lookout-post idea, you have to care deeply about something specific, while absorbed in solving problems that affect others. This is a *sustainable* (long-term) rather than *situational* (short-term) approach to conducting business in the twenty-first century.

Google inspires such a setting, a distinct learning environment, in which small teams of three work together to create lookout-post ideas. Engineers are encouraged to spend 20 percent of their week exploring topics that genuinely interest and excite them, the goal being to generate outside-the-box ideas that lead to innovative projects. Google limits hierarchy, which reduces levels of middle management and attracts the best talent. The company has found that lookout-post ideas develop when employees work in small teams, which keeps Google entrepreneurial instead of bureaucratic and lethargic.

Google won't stop with developing the top search engine in cyberspace. Their mission is "to organize the world's information and make it universally accessible and useful." The company teamed with NASA to create Google maps. It's attempting to become a digital Gutenberg Press by collaborating with libraries in the US and UK, including Oxford and Harvard. Google created a unique scanning system that is not only quick and efficient but also sensitive to original books, which reduces damage to them. The company also understands the need to gain publishers' support and help the industry make money for the virtual library to be successful.

Having access to the world's books offers individuals a new liberty and freedom. My grandmother and great-grandmother never learned to read. Most slaves weren't permitted to read due to the fear that they would grow to think on their own. Now Google is trying to change these millennial-old inequities. Twenty years from now, imagine reading the US Constitution, *The Great Gatsby*, or a bestselling novel on the latest portable gadget in the Sahara Desert at midnight.

Anything is possible.

Google won't stop with the virtual library. The company is exploring the complex science of genes, through expanding databases, swifter search engines, and the development of a gene catalog. Google's Godlike artificial intelligence may one day enable scientists to glean new thinking about the function of genes. Science through cyberspace—the twenty-first-century laboratory—may lead to the production of more affordable energy, such as cutting-edge solar panels, as well as cures for cancer and other diseases.

Google's goals are akin to President John F. Kennedy's call to put a man on the moon by the end of the 1960s. Anything is possible through lookout-post leadership.

The Flip Versus the Freight Train

We've just made it through the "flip" era, a style that encourages the worst of capitalism. The flip model is rushed, myopic, and dangerous—the-Icarus-flying-near-the-sun approach that leads to tragedy.

Nine years ago you could buy a house at a certain price, turn it around in less than a quarter, and make plenty of money. In the flip mode, buyers behave in any way they wish, with few restrictions. This strategy amplifies selfishness. The tragedy is that this crazy business model hurts those of us who didn't participate in the mortgage industry. We spent a decade watching people flip houses, stocks, and derivates. We applauded and envied. But when a few dive into the pool of selfishness, all get wet.

The short-term flip crowd needs lookout-post guidance. An old Nebraskan affectionately nicknamed the Oracle of Omaha invested forty-four billion dollars in a nineteenth-century technology—the freight train.

Crazy, huh?

Warren Buffett never will see his lookout-post idea fully completed because it's a one-hundred-year project, not a quarterly flip. It's massive, akin to the twentieth-century highway project, a major enhancement to the country's transportation system.

Matt Rose, CEO of BNSF Railway, once received a call from Warren Buffett, who said, "I'm looking forward to our first century together." Rose was shocked because his investors had never used the term "century" before. But that's Buffett's lookout-post value, which leads to investing in rational ("arrive in Athens" versus "plunge to the sea") opportunities.

Buffet views freight railroads as our future, and they already have a strong infrastructure in place. US rail was 144 percent more efficient in 2008 than in 1980. Trains can carry massive amounts of freight and travel 457 miles on one gallon of diesel fuel. If 10 percent of freight now moved by truck were moved to rails, the US would burn one billion fewer gallons of fuel a year. Buffett is betting that the use of freight trains will only continue to grow throughout the twenty-first century.

We don't know what's going to happen in the next one hundred years, but it took an eighty-year-old businessman (who came of age during the Depression and World War II) to spot a twenty-first-century opportunity. Buffett sees freight rails as the lowest-cost option for transporting heavy loads across long distances and also recognizes that they would reduce energy costs and increase transportation options in a country with a fast-growing population.

Freight railways are best positioned to grow and don't rely on cash-poor governments to maintain their infrastructure or build new lines, unlike highways and airports. The railways are a back-to-the-future transportation system in terrific shape to move raw material and other products across the nation in a less expensive and more environmentally friendly way.

Buffett is a giraffe-inspired leader who is leading herds back to an old feeding ground where a new crop has been planted. Like Google, Buffett creates smart risks, spending money with thought and concern for more than his company, Berkshire Hathaway. The freight train is the largest investment in the firm's history, and he will likely be dead when the trains become a major part of our country's transportation and financial success.

Buffett is a renaissance man, fully connected to other herds. He sees further down the plains than many others and takes risks that are rooted in his values. He saw the velocity of change and reflected on what works and what doesn't work. He understood that we don't have the money to invest more in the highway system, that the airlines are in the red, but that trains already have a strong infrastructure. He spotted the solution to a vexing transportation and energy problem in the railroads that needed to be invigorated.

The market looks at Buffett as an Oracle of the Future. He is not simply looking out for other billionaires. He's looking out for you and me. His investment in freight rail is like the giraffe bull snorting an alarm to other herbivores, who will break into a gallop to follow him away from crouching lions.

A Lookout Post's Final Warning

In a 2007 interview by Fast Company, MIT's Peter Senge cautioned that even today leadership is parallel to management in the industrial age. We run companies like machines, and "a good machine is one that its operators can control—in the service of its owners' objectives." Senge suggests that "company" is a word that "couldn't be more at odds with the idea of a machine."

Senge defines "company" through the root of the word, the same as "companion" or the "sharing of bread." Twenty-first century leaders need to view organizations not as machines but as living organisms. Machine-run companies hire "mechanics" to keep them running. What the US needs in the future are institutions that are organic—run by humans who are capable of learning, sharing, trusting, and growing.

Senge suggests "gardeners," who nurture life and help it to grow, as another apt metaphor for the twenty-first-century leadership style. As last century's award-winning lookout post, Senge warns that "our industrial-age management, industrial-age organization, and industrial-age way of living...[are] not sustainable."

CHAPTER 2

Gentle Giants—Twenty-First-Century Communication

There exists no less offensive a beast than the giraffe. It lives peaceably with its kind for the most part and bears not the slightest degree of ill-will toward other kinds of animals—both of which, as character recommendations, are more than can be said about the majority of people!

—KEN STOTT, JR., FORMER SAN DIEGO ZOO CURATOR, 1953

We need a fresh leadership model, a twenty-first-century style that contradicts the top-down management approach that hasn't changed much in the past seventy-five years. Leaders must strive to have a positive impact on communities—even on the world, because we're increasingly connected through technology. More than ever in this country's brief 236-year history, business requires leaders who behave like giraffes do in the wild—not simply as alert lookout posts but also as nurturing herbivores, gentle giants who forage peacefully within herds with no distinct alpha male.

My older brothers and I were introduced to this calm yet structured style through our parents while growing up in the 1950s and 1960s. It wasn't simply our parents' words but also their actions that we witnessed and absorbed each day. They cared about us as well as others outside of our immediate family. They listened actively before offering feedback, which led us and others in the community to understand options for dealing with change, continuous learning, and growth.

Our parents knew that when working two—often three—jobs, they lost valuable time to spend with my brothers and me. But they remained positive. Their exposure through work to the growing middle class (my father a janitor in Elmira's public schools, my mother a domestic worker and nurse's aide in a senior citizens' home), helped them realize how vital learning was if their children were to have successful lives. They guided us to be involved in activities outside of our immediate family at the local arts center, The Neighborhood House. They exposed us to youth groups in which we traveled across the Northeast, the South, and regions of the Midwest as passionate members of choirs and sports teams. They were attuned to our challenges and encouraged daily conversations. If our parents sensed we needed others' guidance, they reached out to people in the community for mentors such as a successful teacher or business owner so that we could learn what our options were to either solve a problem or figure out the next step to *move forward* in life.

Raised during the Great Depression, our parents experienced the plight of hunger while waiting in soup lines. Like many of their generation, they appreciated anything they were able to obtain through honest work. As they labored through multiple blue-collar jobs, they found time to support area food kitchens and volunteer for the Boy Scouts. They informally adopted other children during Christmas and on birthdays to ensure that those with less never would have to experience the many dark days they had during the Depression. By focusing on others' birthdays, my parents were dedicated to the notion that every person, especially the young and old, should be recognized, even with a simple card.

These basic values were so engrained in my family and the Elmira community that within two decades I translated my parents' beliefs to my growing role in corporate business, where I discovered that when you honestly offer a gentle nature, you engage people, who over time become committed because they understand that you genuinely care about their well-being. When hard-to-earn trust occurs, people are willing not only to support your direction but also contribute innovative ideas.

The *millennial children* are a strong example of the urgent need for this leadership style, a twenty-something demographic that futurists feel embrace the concept of "the fallen of the priesthood." These kids aren't easy to sway. They aren't in awe because you own a company or run a law firm that bears your name. They aren't as impressed with societal emperors such as executives, politicians, or entertainment legends. Most of these kids feel that you're blessed to have them work for you.

Many corporate HR departments chase the millennials, even luring them to Disney World on recruiting trips. Many leaders entice this demographic by offering flexible work hours, but often this is a trap because the majority of change is superficial; if millennials don't make billable hours, they're in trouble just as they would be in the industrial age.

Since World War II, the emergence of more participative and inclusive management styles hasn't resulted in authentic, nurturing work environments. Most companies and leaders aren't truly committed to this model. The tragedy is that these companies claim they're progressive and inclusive and promote all of the modern-day concepts of a flexible workforce, teamwork, and employee training and development, but deep down there's little change. As soon as a product fails to reach its goal, a strategy doesn't work, or a basic objective isn't achieved, management reverses to the primal role of self-preservation. Then, loyalty to the employee is abandoned. The consequence is that employees instinctively feel that lack of commitment and immediately seek their own self-preservation—a cycle that must end as soon as possible.

Reduce the Machiavellians

The failure of the Machiavellian leadership style is that employees are viewed as puppets to be manipulated. There's little sensitivity to employee needs except for the monetary and the egotistic, which are used as negative tools for motivation, a fundamental weakness of the style since it does not bond employees to the organization or to one another. It creates a "What's in it for me?" mentality, and when a crisis occurs, employees bail to save themselves instead of holding on to help save the company.

In the late 1980s, I worked at US Home—one of the largest US builders and one of the fastest-growing companies that employed the rigid Machiavellian model. We were instructed to split into groups and perform weekly reviews of books about management and leadership style.

It was an indoctrination, a process designed to create a sense of allegiance and loyalty to the company. The aim was to get everyone on the management team together and preach the US Home doctrine. We had a week to review each book then return to groups and chat about the book's value and relevance to the mission of US Home. We had to visit a psychiatrist and take a battery of exams to ensure that we met a culture-dictated profile. The company clearly wanted employees to know they were insignificant and had few rights.

US Home rewarded its employees for following top-down rules and goals. Construction workers were awarded contracts for building a home in less than nine weeks without concern for quality. Salespeople were motivated to sell regardless of the buyer's eligibility or their genuine concern for the customers' needs. These rewards led to poor construction, which resulted in major lawsuits stemming from leaking roofs and deteriorating dry walls that had been improperly installed. Because US Home had relationships with mortgage companies, they could influence approval decisions from a "no" to "yes," which led many customers to purchase homes they couldn't afford, a precursor to what happened with subprime loans in the past decade. We were pressured to meet the company profile; conformity was the theme of the day. An irony is that even though US Home was one of the fastest-growing builders at that time, even making it to the prestigious Fortune 500 company list, it was also the swiftest to disappear.

Nothing about this leadership style says, "I like you."

As an employee, I felt owned, manipulated—never supported. We had to say we were sitting on the company chair or writing at the company desk or speaking on the company phone, a distinctive trait of the Machiavellian style. One vice president was so frustrated by feeling controlled that he bought his own furniture to try to overcome the defeating setting.

Communication for a New Century

In contrast to the Machiavellian style—which hasn't faded quickly enough—is the leadership shown by former NFL head coach Tony Dungy of the Indianapolis Colts. Now here's a man who is a respected, successful leader and a decent human being to boot.

And that's key.

Tony Dungy's not only intelligent and kind but also determined to win and committed to seeing players develop so they can achieve too. He's a leader in a multimillion-dollar industry, equivalent to the CEO on the field. Unlike the yelling and sarcastic, I'm-the-leader-you're-the-follower style of Vince Lombardi or Mike Ditka, Dungy adopted an unsullied approach that a variety of managers and progressive businesses are recognizing and slowly beginning to embrace.

Dungy's leadership style is more appropriate for the millennial generation who won't worship the priesthood, those in power with lofty-sounding titles. Today's leaders must engage this demographic internally to earn its trust. While he was an NFL coach, Dungy respected every stakeholder from the ball boy and referee, to the players and owner. He offered a collaborative culture where all felt safe to perform their jobs; he replaced the NFL's hierarchical structure, which relied on fear as a motivator to victory. ESPN reported that Dungy set league records for most consecutive playoff seasons (ten) and consecutive twelve-win seasons (six), and has the highest average of regular-season victories of any coach in league history (10.7).

Dungy continues to lead as a sports television analyst because he's a keen observer, a student of the game, and a former coach who discovers ways to bring people into a shared goal versus ordering them into the process. Viewers enjoy his refreshing nature and educational analysis of the sport. He strives to be an objective critic—not to beat down the subject of his evaluation (the team, coach, or player). He provides constructive insights and uses his position of broadcaster to elevate others, even in the studio, which contrasts with many of his peers' often condescending comments throughout televised games.

A significant benefit of Dungy's leadership style appeared after he left the Colts in 2009. His assistant coaches easily took over the team and continued to win because of Dungy's shared leadership, which had included them in the larger process of coaching an NFL team through seven years of victory. His staff remained competitive and earned another trip to the Super Bowl in 2010.

There's a distinct parallel between Tony Dungy and corporate America.

Business leaders need to engage various groups of people by removing their dated industrial style to fit our times. This shift requires a genuine commitment to employees and customers by taking a respectful approach that offers encouraging words and creates a calm, productive setting that embraces a teaching philosophy. Twenty-first century leadership is an option, a selection, an intrinsic value.

It won't work if it's veneer.

A dramatic example of this subtle leadership style was demonstrated by US Airways pilot, Captain "Sully" Sullenberger, a man who spent his life laboring in a setting of obscurity, where each day he patiently learned more about his field. Sully earned a bachelor's degree in psychology and two master's degrees, one in industrial psychology and one in public administration. He performed accident investigation duties for the U.S. Air Force and served as an Air Line Pilots Association (ALPA) representative during a National Transportation Safety Board Investigation. He also is an educator, who developed and taught a Crew Resource Management course to hundreds of airline crewmembers.

A Sully leadership highlight began during the tense, terrifying moments in the sky over Manhattan in January 2009. He could have panicked or given up, yet his calm, focused approach prevented loss. Sully relaxed in wisdom gleaned from decades of professional learning that came together in 208 miraculous minutes for the benefit of his passengers and crew.

What if global companies hired thousands of Sullys each decade instead of a half-dozen per century? What would be the tangible results? How would this affect the US and the world as we *move forward* in this century?

Like the giraffe that leads the famished herd to a grove of acacia trees, Sully cared deeply about his passengers and crew. He led with acutely focused actions that were rooted in lifelong professional learning and universal values for others, which produced spectacular results—the smooth landing of the Airbus A320 on the chilly Hudson River, the only space available near the towering New York City metropolis.

Like Dungy and Sully, I try to mirror this fresh style of communication that I hope one day replaces the old I'm-the-police officer-and-you're-the-crook discussion that appears when one feels a sense of deep control over others. In 2000, when I headed up a subsidiary at PricewaterhouseCoopers (PwC), the employees had been through three CEOs in nine months. It was a new period in which outsourcing was becoming common. The atmosphere made employees feel that soon their jobs would be lost too, which created a stressful, turbulent period in their lives. They learned not to trust anyone and therefore couldn't believe in anyone.

At one of our first meetings, I deliberately sat on the floor and asked the seated staff to rise—a simple yet symbolic gesture. I wanted them to understand that I wasn't standing above them, glaring down, commanding. My leadership would be focused on supporting them to become leaders themselves, so they could advance their professional lives during a frightening period (that bump) in their careers.

They were former employees of Equifax, a successful Fortune 500 company and a legendary name in credit reporting before they had been transferred to PricewaterhouseCoopers. Equifax was a stodgy, traditional organization, an environment in which you called sharply dressed executives "Mr." or "Ms." and rarely saw or had contact with them since they kept to their exclusive C-level domains.

During my first few weeks, I met with customers and evaluated the Equifax management style. While PwC was attempting to transform this style, the company was still focused on the importance of titles such as "partner."

Anyone below was not as important.

I wanted the employees to understand that I wasn't like other CEOs or their recent bosses at Equifax. I deliberately sat on the floor to symbolize that I was there to serve them. My leadership style was predicated on nurturing them in a sincere effort to further their success, which would be my success too.

Imagine two hundred people seated in a spacious room after being served a wonderful lunch only to see their new CEO sitting in a suit on the floor, explaining why they mattered. Most had rarely met C-level executives and could not call them by their first names. They were used to treating executives as royalty, whereas I conveyed that I was a common person too.

They looked shocked, staring down where I sat before responding with a round of applause that lasted for several minutes. That first day together felt as though we had received a proclamation of emancipation. We were bound to one another now as we attempted to *rise* after a serious corporate *fall* and devise a plan to continue to *move forward* and feed.

The Patient Before Commerce

This authentically caring style of communication isn't limited to coaches and pilots; it's even appearing today in the profit-driven pharmaceutical field. Novartis is one of the largest pharmaceutical companies on the planet. Its creative, giraffe-inspired CEO, Dan Vasella, is a Swiss-born medical doctor with years of experience working closely with patients. In our intensive, quarterly-driven climate (where short-term goals are the top prize), it's refreshing to hear about the CEO of Novartis focus on solving tricky, long-term problems for doctors and their patients.

By working in smaller markets and exploring new drugs, Vasella built his company. From the start, he chose not to lead by focusing on developing blockbuster drugs or instituting early marketing analysis in an effort to reap major profits in the short term. Instead Vasella concentrated on long-term research and development to create innovative drugs that addressed medical needs, improving the health of human beings—the medical field's herd.

Like Captain Sully Sullenberger, Vasella is a sharp example of the twenty-first-century leadership archetype, which communicates caring foremost. When asked during the *Washington Post's* "On Leadership" interview by Steve Pearlstein whether Novartis exists for investors or to create new medicines for patients, Vasella responded, "If you do fulfill your purpose in society…deliver what customers, in this case patients, perceive as value, you will also generate profits.... But if you run after profits and you run after the money, you forget for what you are really here for."

Vasella never has forgotten who he is, a medical doctor who wants to discover innovative medicines to treat people with illness. For more than two thousand years, the medical field has had an ethical standard for doctors—the Hippocratic Oath. Even though the medical community didn't live up to these standards for centuries, the ideals that focused on people were established and taught and refined for the next generation, then the next, and the next.

These *giraffe*-inspired traits mirrored in the Hippocratic Oath's ethics are also appearing in business schools today. Recently the Harvard MBA program enacted an oath that may encourage ethical traits of caring for others.

The Harvard MBA Oath

As a business leader I recognize my role in society.

My purpose is to lead people and manage resources to create value that no single individual can create alone.

My decisions affect the well-being of individuals inside and outside my enterprise, today and tomorrow.

Therefore, I promise that:

I will manage my enterprise with loyalty and care, and will not advance my personal interests at the expense of my enterprise or society.

I will understand and uphold, in letter and spirit, the laws and contracts governing my conduct and that of my enterprise.

I will refrain from corruption, unfair competition, or business practices harmful to society.

I will protect the human rights and dignity of all people affected by my enterprise, and I will oppose discrimination and exploitation.

I will protect the right of future generations to advance their standard of living and enjoy a healthy planet.

I will report the performance and risks of my enterprise accurately and honestly.

I will invest in developing myself and others, helping the management profession continue to advance, and create sustainable and inclusive prosperity.

In exercising my professional duties according to these principles, I recognize that my behavior must set an example of integrity, eliciting trust and esteem from those I serve. I will remain accountable to my peers and to society for my actions and for upholding these standards.

This oath I make freely, and upon my honor.

Many criticize this type of oath because honoring it will require significant change from the industrial-age management model. The oath asks for a leadership style that is socially aware, humane, and fair—especially in profit-based business environments.

The Harvard oath is a *lookout-post* goal designed to inspire (not force) the ethics taught at universities that are often abandoned once the MBA graduate arrives in a cacophonous, rushed, and paradoxical work setting. The oath is a *lookout-post* warning. It's prescient, a goal for business to act as a true profession (versus a semi-profession), one with ethical standards that in reality not all will meet, but the majority, over time (such as those in medicine and law), will strive to weave into their working lives, which will lead to a stronger, more respected, and influential profession—vital to success in the increasingly open knowledge age.

In the article "Harvard Changes Course," Harvard Business School Dean Nitin Nohria says that after the 2008 financial crisis "the public lost trust in business, and some of our graduates seem to be responsible for that." Harvard's reputation was stained by the financial crisis, so the university acted by restructuring its curriculum through new, required courses that focus on ethics and teamwork. The goal is to develop "leaders of competence and character, rather than just connections and credentials," adds Brian Kenny, the university's chief marketing officer.

Open Versus Closed Leadership

Nurturing traits that lead to trust are not only found in relationships between employers and employees in the twenty-first century. Today companies and CEOs must take a more engaging approach with customers. We must end the unilateral approach that occasionally offers a survey or focus group and *move forward* to provide a more interactive Web 2.0 approach that figuratively puts the customer on the board of advisors.

The US endured the values of the 1960s *Mad Men* with the dominant "me" attitude. Back then the consumer was considered to be stupid. The *Mad Men* told the consumer to go buy Tide because it was the best product, and the consumer had few options but to go buy Tide as directed.

Consumer trust (rather than fear) is vital to consumers when making selections today and will continue to grow because technology is an enabler. To buy a car, house, vacuum cleaner, or even a garden hose, most seek advice from friends to gather trusted information about where to go and what to watch for so that they don't get gutted by the lingering *Mad Men* out there.

There's fresh evidence that change is occurring with small businesses and international corporations shifting their focus from just selling to seeking out what truly helps customers. The company Simplisafe launched an inexpensive way to offer wireless security systems to apartment tenants, a product that works with cell phones and allows renters (who previously never had an inexpensive security option) to take the product with them when they move.

Bornfree, which produces BPA-free bottles, continues to innovate for the least-powerful on earth—babies—by offering a venting system that reduces the air infants suck in as they drink a bottle, while also decreasing irritation and even the risk of illness.

Darn Tough Vermont took on the sock industry by creating a sports sock using "merino wool and more stitches per inch than rivals." Even though the cost is fifteen to twenty dollars per pair, the product has a lifetime guarantee and is popular due to the socks' fit, comfort, and durability. Creating better socks for intensely active customers has contributed to two-thirds of Darn Tough Vermont's revenue.

In the CNN.com article "Can P&G Make Money in Places Where People Earn $2 a Day?" Jennifer Reingold reports that on the corporate side Procter and Gamble (P&G) has invested money in research and development to learn more about the world's poor, a developing market that's increasing from 6 percent to 8 percent annually, whereas the developed world market is rising more slowly—from 1 percent to 2 percent in 2011. CEO and Chairman Robert McDonald said that P&G's long-term goal consists of "touching and improving more lives, in more parts of the world, more completely" in a sincere effort to increase "purpose-inspired growth."

It's a lookout-post idea that requires the company to spend more research and development money to continue to learn about the world's poor, the underserved, and customers who earn two dollars each day. P&G researchers helped to reduce stereotypes after they spent time in homes in countries such as Brazil, China, and India. They discovered that the poor don't want simple products but aspire for access to products such as those created for the middle class and the rich. Since they spend hours outside, they need low-cost skin-care products and shampoo rather than the harsh soap they've used for decades. They too wish to look beautiful at that future job interview.

P&G is taking an anthropological research method instead of the historical we-build-it-and-they-will-come marketing approach. Today P&G gets a third of its sales from developing regions, up from 20 percent in 2000. CEO Robert McDonald wants to raise that percentage to 50 percent by 2020. This revenue wouldn't have shown up on the company's spreadsheets if P&G's leaders hadn't invested time and money to learn more about the needs of the world's poor.

The Captain, Cook, Correspondent, and Oiler

When I read the short story "The Open Boat" by Stephen Crane, the turn-of-the-twentieth-century tale stood out because it offered a sharp narrative about the importance of *caring* leadership.

The ship's captain leads his crew after a terrible *fall*—the sinking of his steamer ship—to the safety of land after spending several days and nights struggling to survive in the frigid January water off the Florida coast.

The captain is injured. He can't row, but he remains alert and patient, despite the dangerous waves pouring into the small lifeboat. As the crew endures nature's violent winds and high waves, along with circling sharks and the fatigue of continuous rowing to shore, the captain always speaks in a low voice.

He offers directions with phrases such as "Keep 'er a little more south, Billie," or "Take her easy now, boys.... Don't spend yourselves. If we have to run a surf, you'll need all your strength, because we'll sure have to swim for it. Take your time."

The captain offers lookout-post ideas such as attempting to sail by using his overcoat at the end of an oar, which gives the rowers much needed rest. Crane describes what the captain creates through nurturing leadership as being "the subtle brotherhood of men that was here established on the seas. No one said it that it was so. No one mentioned it. But it dwelt in the boat, and each man felt it warm him."

After days of dealing with the messy environment of a life-threatening sea (a picture that would look beautiful from land but would be an ugly image if you were sitting inside a tiny boat fighting not to drown), the men realize they need one another to survive the indifference of nature, which doesn't care whether they survive or die.

Despite the stressful setting, the men don't get angry or yell at one another. One night as a cold wave rushes across the bow, the captain says serenely, "Bail her, Cook."

"All right, Captain," says the cheerful cook.

The story reveals how caring leadership always has been available. Read literature or history or any religious tome, and you'll spot it. The problem today is that we've belittled humane leadership, jamming it into the box of stereotypes by labeling it as childlike or naive. But it's much harder to stay calm and nurturing during tragedies and falls when people need to come together to survive, and Crane's conclusion offers more.

Out of the crew's four men, the oiler is the most muscular, the healthiest, and the most energetic. So when the captain attempts a run to land through powerful shoreline waves, the oiler leaps off the boat just as it is being swamped, electing to swim away from the boat, alone, confident in his strength to beat nature, while the cook, correspondent, and captain stay near one another, communicating as they wrestle with the strong surf and life-threatening currents.

The injured captain uses one hand to cling to the back of the boat and continues to guide the crew to shore. When he spots the cook struggling, even though the cook has a life-ring around his core, the captain calls to him, "Turn over on your back, Cook! Turn over on your back and use the oar!"

The cook soon paddles and moves "ahead as if he were a canoe."

Meanwhile, the correspondent is stuck in a rip current but can hear the captain calling for him to "Come to the boat!" which is parallel to the shore. As the correspondent responds and swims to the captain, "a large wave caught him and flung him with ease and supreme speed completely over the boat and far beyond it... [arriving] in water that reached only his waist."

The captain's subtle leadership from the moment of the ship's sinking to arriving on land is never veneer. He is alert, looking out for the crew even when injured and psychologically dealing with a major *fall* in his profession (the rare shipwreck).

One of the story's timeless themes centers around how humans think they can control nature or life's successes or failures, but usually they can't. Think about experiencing that sudden hurricane, earthquake, tornado, or blizzard. The best way to survive any of life's complexities is to understand that people working together is much more powerful than people working alone, the way humans always have dealt with nature's indifference regarding whether we live or die.

The cook, correspondent, and captain survive the arduous journey through the winter sea even though they're the physically weakest members of the crew, while the oiler—the strongest—swims off alone and drowns.

CHAPTER 3

A Violent Birth—The Cycle of Falls and Rises

After fifteen months in the womb...babies, or calves, are born headfirst and drop six feet to the ground from the standing mom. Boom. Welcome to Earth... It is usually up on its own spindly legs within an hour, a vital defense against a hungry enemy.

—LYNN SHERR, JOURNALIST, 1997

Giraffes are vulnerable at birth. The event is a rude awakening, a survival test, and a rough-and-tumble introduction onto the plains of Africa. The calf drops from its mother's pouch, building speed that severs the umbilical cord. As the calf flails on the ground, a powerful image hovers above, providing a moment of calm when the newborn has a decision to make—*Do I lie still or rise to join my mother standing before me?*

People experience *falls* too, both physical and emotional. My dear friend and former colleague, Robert Carter, graduated from college in 1971 and began work as a CPA at the Big Eight firm of

Ernst and Young in Fort Worth, Texas. There were no other black auditors in the office at that time, and fewer than fifty African Americans across the country worked at prestigious national accounting firms such as Ernst and Young. Adding to Robert's disappointment, most clients at the Fort Worth office felt uncomfortable hiring a black man to work on their accounts. Many openly said they didn't want Robert around.

What illuminated Robert's *fall* occurred at a local country club event. Robert and his wife were prevented from entering a banquet room reserved for "whites only." They stood staring as Robert's peers and spouses walked past without saying a word before they entered the early-seventies, segregated room. Robert reacted with an intense mix of embarrassment, humiliation, and frustration that swiftly turned into anger.

As when a giraffe is violently born, Robert struck the ground shortly after entering the accounting profession, a dream job that he had struggled to secure after being raised in a Southern, poor, blue-collar family. At the office he received scant encouragement, his professional network limited because he had few college-educated friends or relatives who could offer much needed advice.

After his *fall*, however, Robert decided he could struggle to his feet as if the world owed him something, or he could calmly rise with an acute focus on learning from the stressful—yet common—experience.

The Value of Genuine (Versus Veneer) Networks

Robert grew up in a small Texas town, a Jim Crow environment where his family picked cotton. He attended all-black schools in a segregated district. Even in his youth, Robert knew that during his life he'd experience falls that would require that he stand tall and move beyond obstacles of race and class. His parents raised six children and stressed that they'd all attend college, a familial lookout-post goal. So when Robert fell in Fort Worth, he knew he had to stand up. The image of that parental giraffe hovering above, encouraging him to *rise*, was prominent in his mind.

All of us need others' encouragement to stand after falls and discover a plan of where to head next. Although his father was not formally educated, Robert had observed his dad's innate talent to repair cars and run a successful family business, leveraging the steady cash flow to invest in his children's education. Robert spent years laboring in the family garage, where he focused on his father's independence rather than the limitations of Jim Crow. His father's work ethic, linked to entrepreneurial success, established a belief in Robert that it's always possible to *rise* from a *fall*, even a powerful, ongoing one like those endured due to Jim Crow practices.

In high school, Robert spotted a path forward through attaining a college education that helped him move beyond the restrictions of the South. He understood that despite the passage of the 1960s civil rights laws, not much had changed in the short term. The alienation in Fort Worth was subtle, lingering racism. So when Fort Worth and the country club scene arrived that evening, Robert experienced an awakening.

He left Ernst and Young for the progressive company Xerox, where he focused on his goal to learn as much as possible about corporate accounting so that in the future he could own a business and become financially independent. Xerox was one of the first companies to promote affinity groups that helped minorities (women, blacks, and Hispanics) to gain access to one another, to gird one another, and to create a culture that welcomed them within the traditional corporate milieu. A key benefit was that members of affinity groups were given access to senior executives. Robert regularly met with numerous diverse and non-diverse Xerox executives, including Barry Rand, now president of AARP, who encouraged him to soar beyond the challenges of society by creating diverse *herds* to support him. Robert was coached through entrepreneurial concepts and leadership development. Eventually he became a Xerox division controller.

Despite his embarrassment at Ernst and Young in Fort Worth, Robert wanted to learn how to work effectively with those who'd knocked him down. At Xerox he was assertive in reaching out to senior managers, directors, and executives for advice that helped navigate him through a new culture called "corporate America." Historically this culture had been restricted to white males. Even most women were excluded at the time. Robert also joined the local rotary club, was introduced to other corporate executives, and continued to learn the ins and outs of corporate America.

Robert never asked these connections for direct help but rather for guidance regarding how to *rise* after a serious *fall*. He became an engaged reader of management books; he helped his peers and those who worked under him as division controller, sharing lessons from corporate leaders to assist with their success too. I met Robert at an interview when he was director of internal audit for an oil and gas company. He reached out to me, offering advice that led us to a productive relationship that has lasted more than twenty-five years.

Ironically the culture that knocked Robert down soon became his *support*. He never sought revenge after Fort Worth but instead opted to treat corporate America like an untidy setting that had disrespected him but also offered wonderful opportunities if he were active in discovering them. He shifted his goal from becoming an accountant to leading a company one day. Patiently he created an authentic network within the corporate community that nurtured him, and in 1983 he launched his own business, Enterprise Advisory Services, Inc. (EASI) in Houston.

Today EASI wins multimillion-dollar contracts from federal agencies and corporate clients. The company weathered the downturns (*falls*) in the Texas economy during the 1980s and '90s due to the oil glut and energy downturn, but balanced its portfolio to remain viable and resilient. Robert will retire soon and plans to go to law school so he can continue to advocate for others.

The Democracy of Technology to Rise and Move Forward

Disease triggered Dr. Elaine Smokewood's *fall* from the safety of the academic womb. She'd once disparaged technology, but after the life-altering diagnosis of Lou Gehrig's disease, she was forced to embrace twenty-first-century gadgets that enabled her to continue her passion of teaching literature and creative writing at Oklahoma City University.

In the 2010 article "Taught by a Terrible Disease," published in *The Chronicle of Higher Education,* Jeffrey Young reports that as Dr. Smokewood's illness progressed, she lost her voice, which was vital to her work in the classroom, and soon she was dropped from teaching face-to-face courses. To stand, Elaine embraced the Web cam linked to a large classroom monitor to visually interact with students, communicating through typed text or a speech synthesizer from her home office.

Dr. Smokewood's classroom role changed as well. Her *fall* helped her recognize that she'd behaved like the majority of professors, as if they were the most important person in the room. She saw her old style of lecturing as a performance, an act she had repeated because the professorial persona or "face that she keeps in a jar by the door" provided an appropriate distance between her and students. She explains:

> *I became a different kind of teacher than I had ever been—I became a teacher who actively listened.... I had in the past often confused listening with waiting for my students to stop talking so that I might resume the very important business of performing.... I learned that if I listened carefully, thoughtfully, generously, and non-judgmentally, my students would delight me with the complexity of their thinking, the depth of their insight, the delicious wickedness of their humor, and with their compassion, their wisdom, and their honesty.*

During her rise from a serious illness with the aid of technology, Dr. Smokewood dramatically altered her teaching style and feels her students learn more now than with the centuries-old university model.

Although Dr. Smokewood lost her voice, she's a better communicator now. She improved as a teacher through the challenging yet engaging process of *falls* and *rises.* Today she's switched roles with students, who've become co-teachers while she's become a co-student, and together they continue to *move forward.*

My college buddy, Leonard Morris, is another example of someone who has benefitted from technology. He was my technical advisor at USC in the 1970s. Leonard taught me not to fear technology but to embrace it. As a college freshman, I learned to view fresh technology through an emotional lens. Like Dr. Elaine Smokewood struggling with ALS, I witnessed how technology could radically improve someone's life. At the age of eighteen, I spotted how the democracy of technology made Leonard competitive. We take for granted the speed of technological advancement: the voice-directed equipment that speaks to us in cars, the hyperconnectedness of wireless gadgets, and the six degrees of separation (reduced to two) because of Facebook, LinkedIn, Twitter, and YouTube.

During the pre-1990s, only major organizations such as General Motors or Princeton University had the money to pay for expensive access to customer information; they could support certain services or penetrate various markets. But with the advent of technology, such as mobile computing, a small company has access to consumers for a nominal cost in a creative manner that's more effective than paying Madison Avenue ad agencies. States such as South Carolina can use Google Maps to make the service of finding public deeds and conducting various real estate transactions with state-of-the-art technology often more effectively than larger states, who are besieged with legacy systems. Technology allows for equal footing, helping to expand an authentic democracy.

My friend Leonard lost his sight at age seven in Detroit, Michigan, but early on he sought the latest technology: a clock that spoke to him, a portable Braille writer so he could take notes, and a mini-cassette recorder to review class lectures. He relied on technology for emotional connectivity. He volunteered his services at associations for the blind where he experimented with unusual technology designed to help the visually impaired, and Leonard reported back whether or not they had value.

Like Dr. Elaine Smokewood, Leonard used technology to learn after one of life's frequent *falls* rather than maintain the norm of remaining static. At our dorm, students sought his guidance before purchasing a stereo, and if Leonard approved, they'd buy it in a jiff. He became our reference guide by owning devices before they became mainstream; it was as if I'd hung around someone who lived in the 1970s yet worked with gadgets from the Jetson era.

I was moved by how technology reduced the gap between the sighted and unsighted. It instilled a sensitivity in me of how technology doesn't discriminate; I saw how wonderfully imagined, equal-opportunity devices helped Leonard transcend his early disability. Leonard never would picture himself walking the streets with that familiar seeing-eye dog. He strived to perform in life like any ordinary person, seeking a mainstream career and lifestyle. His nightmare was that over time he would continue to *fall*, ending up selling candy each morning at the Detroit train station. But after graduating from USC in 1978 with the aid of cutting-edge technology, Leonard saw his nightmare vanish when he went to work for the government as an IT specialist, an engaging career that lasted until 2006 when he retired from the California Department of Motor Vehicles as a manager in policy and information.

Technology, however, not only sparks *rises* but also triggers *falls.*

In 1912, Lillian Gish showcased her first-rate acting talent in silent films. But soon a shift in technology radically changed her profession. Gish responded (nearly one hundred years ago) in a way we need to embrace today. She accepted change even though it would cause stress and eliminate the silent acting field in which she was recognized as a major star through films such as *The Birth of a Nation* (1915) and *Orphans of the Storm* (1921).

Most of Gish's fellow actors bluntly rejected the transition from silent film to sound, but she had a conviction to learn new skills in a field that was experiencing a West Coast earthquake. She transferred her talents to the stage in the play *Hamlet* (1936) and talkies such as *Duel in the Sun* (1946), for which she was nominated for the Academy Award for Best Supporting Actress.

The result of *rising* after a career *fall* was that Gish not only kept her job but also contributed to her field for more than half of century. In 1971 she earned a special Academy Award for "superlative artistry and for distinguished contribution to the progress of motion pictures." Gish was that rare person who not only accepted but also embraced change, living to the age of ninety-nine and dying in her sleep of natural causes.

Change ain't easy—most of us spend much of our lives fighting these shifts that arrive like tides on the beach. Perhaps a giraffe-inspired approach is best, one in which we accept falls as Lillian Gish did by knowing they often stimulate growth if we elect to stand and join a *new herd* while continuing to learn from an industry collapse, a wise response in our new century of shifts that occur through technology.

Never Fear Falls

When we earnestly believe in something to pursue in life, *falls* should make us more determined. It's like getting the training wheels taken off your bike as a kid when your parents encouraged you to ride that bike like the older children in the neighborhood. You *fell* but didn't let the scrapes, bruises, and embarrassment stop you; instead you were committed to climbing back on that shiny red bike.

Each of us has a unique approach when dealing with falls, but the key is to turn the sudden drop into a moment of opportunity and commitment. We can't prepare for every shift in life, so we need to stop fearing falls and instead embrace them. My father worked at the Chemung Foundry, a steel mill that made parts for various industrial machines. In 1957 the plant closed, and all the employees lost their jobs and pensions. This was prior to federal laws (the ERISA Act of 1974) that protected pensions. After twenty years of work, my father shifted from a high-paying job to unemployment while dealing with recent debt due to having bought a better house in an all-white neighborhood.

His *fall* was stressful, but he soon found a job as a janitor in the Elmira School District, which paid him only half of his foundry salary. Based on experiencing a lifetime of falls, my father instinctively knew how to stand and leverage the drop. He was creative and optimistic and had a sense of purpose. He used the new job to start a well-paying cleaning business on the side for wealthy doctors and lawyers in Elmira, which helped him pay his mortgage and other expenses.

As a school janitor, my father gave me access to books and advice from teachers, counselors, and administrators he befriended. He brought home discarded encyclopedias for me to study. He encouraged other students to keep learning and believing in themselves. His midcareer fall led him to engage in a new job, launch a side business, and increase his fatherly role while helping others in the community. What struck me at his funeral was when people from varied demographics said how my father had made a difference in their lives. Now that's a *rise* after a midcareer *fall.*

Embrace Failure and Success

Studies reveal that failure is increasingly common today due to the speed of change triggered by twenty-first-century technology. The average time a company spends in the S&P 500 Index has dropped from seventy-five years in 1937 to approximately fifteen years today. Yet failure also can be a form of creativity. If a company goes bankrupt in Silicon Valley, it is often a sign of courage. Thomas Edison engaged in nine thousand experiments before producing the successful new technology called the light bulb that we still use today. Today many companies have failure parties or an annual prize for the best failed idea. During reviews at P&G, employees discuss successes and failures as though they're equal.

The irony is that success can be as difficult as failure to *rise* from and *move forward* after. *Falls* and *rises* are more intertwined than most people understand. Successful sports coaches often advise players that it's best to lose earlier in the season in order to win later in the playoffs.

Why?

Because most companies use success as emotional stimulation rather than as a learning technique—a twenty-first-century mistake. Success often breeds a cozy environment where the ego concludes, "I know it all." Success usually doesn't trigger reflection, and what's most dangerous is that success, like failure, can lead to a static, non-learning environment for organizations and employees.

Apple is a recent example of how smart companies link failure and success. Like failure, success must bring authentic reflection and change, not simply repetition, because in the twenty-first century that's not enough to stay current. Through strong reflection of success, *falls* are often reduced and guide companies to opportunities for extended growth.

In the 1990s, Apple failed with the Newton tablet, yet the company learned from the Newton *fall* and continued to focus on the long-term goal of creating a portable tablet. In the short term, though, Apple took a smaller risk by creating the iPhone in 2007, which was—and continues to be—wildly successful.

Apple continued to learn from both the Newton failure and the iPhone success, treating them as equal, relevant, and vital research to gather information for the company to reflect upon before taking a smarter risk—creating the iPad, another substantial victory that continues today. The result of treating both success and failure, much as a doctor treats disease, helped Apple to jump up to number one, overtaking Google as the world's most valuable brand; in August 2012 Apple was cited as the most valuable company in history by *Forbes*.

Former Federal Reserve chairman Allan Greenspan contradicts Apple's insightful approach to change. He's an example of how strong success can give birth to a non-learning environment that over time leads to major *falls*. Years of economic success made Greenspan overconfident in financial models (or dinosaur theories) that weren't updated until the 2008 financial collapse and near economic meltdown.

From 1992 to 2008, the US experienced unprecedented growth (with some dips), but we had "full" employment. Greenspan said this model would continue. He didn't keep reflecting on success or ask basic questions such as "Is there more we can do to improve our models? Was it serendipity or the new global economy that caused our success, events we didn't influence?"

Greenspan felt his model was structured so well that he repeated it, a behavior encircled in the dangerous "success belief."

Greenspan embraced classical economics, which said that you stimulate growth and control it by managing interest rates and the money supply. Classical economics, however, did not anticipate the global community that supports a global economy. The classical economists were so comfortable in their success that they could not see the 2008 global meltdown coming. The collapse proved that changing, complex, interconnected, and codependent economies will require a new approach rather than a static one as we continue to attempt to rise from the 2008 fall. Greenspan later conceded that he was surprised that his once successful models had failed.

As with the example of Apple, engaging in critical thinking and ongoing experiments after success is crucial to further success and can reduce *falls*. Companies must test theories by routinely and objectively asking, "Why did it work?"

The Great American Fall—Willy Versus Charlie, Biff Versus Bernard

More than sixty years after Arthur Miller's play *Death of a Salesman* debuted on Broadway in 1949, the American tragedy thematically raises questions that are perhaps more pertinent today and link to my call for giraffe-inspired leadership.

Willy Loman is a lifelong, traveling salesman, who believes in the saying "Be liked and you will never want." Willy teaches these simple "be popular" values to his sons, Biff and Hap, as a way to achieve gigantic success versus living the life of their nerdy next-door neighbor and childhood friend, Bernard. Willy lectures his boys throughout the play:

> *Bernard can get the best marks in school y'understand, but when he gets out in the business world, y'understand, you are going to be five times ahead of him. That's why I thank Almighty God you're both built like Adonises. Because the man who makes an appearance in the business world, the man who creates personal interest is the man who gets ahead. Be liked and you will never want.*

Life's successes, however, aren't that tidy, particularly in the second half of the information age. Willy never has earned a lot of money, even though it's his goal. "Be liked and you will not want" doesn't work in the long term, perhaps more so today. We need to bring much more to our careers in the twenty-first century.

Years later, Biff and his younger brother, Hap (who follows Willy's vision of personality over knowledge), are living disastrous lives. Biff never attended college, even though he had three athletic scholarships. He cheated on tests, stole from stores, and even spent time in prison. Hap, patterning his life after Willy's, is a womanizer and habitual liar. He has unrealistic short-term dreams and is not reflective as he tries to climb the slippery corporate ladder. The reality—which Hap can't see—is that he isn't a CEO but an assistant's assistant.

In contrast, Bernard's father, Charlie (Willy's neighbor and closest friend), has developed a successful business over years that he never brags about, while raising Bernard with values that contradict Willy's.

Charlie never preached that an attractive personality alone would move his son to the top of the steep, slippery ladder. Instead, Charlie let Bernard decide what he wished to do in life and led his son by a concrete example that there are no shortcuts to career success. It's never guaranteed. Charlie knew Bernard would have a stronger chance for attaining success and negotiating through life's necessary *falls* if Bernard chose to work hard at something he felt passionate about, which would lead to ongoing learning through a natural engagement.

At a chance meeting at Charlie's office late in the play, Willy says to the now adult Bernard:

"I'm—I'm overjoyed to see how you made the grade, Bernard, overjoyed. It's an encouraging thing to see a young man really—really—Looks very good for Biff—very—(he breaks off, then) Bernard—(He is so full of emotion, he breaks off again.)
Bernard: What is it, Willy?
Willy (small and alone): What—what's the secret?"

Bernard: What secret?
Willy: How—how did you? Why didn't he ever catch on?
Bernard: I wouldn't know that, Willy.
Willy: (confidentially, desperately): You were his friend, his boyhood friend. There's something I don't understand about it. His life ended after that Ebbets Field game. From the age of seventeen nothing good ever happened to him.
Bernard: He never trained himself for anything.

Throughout the play, Willy keeps asking his dead uncle, Ben; his neighbor, Charlie; and now Charlie's son, Bernard, how they became successful.

None of them answer Willy with a formula to follow, which is what Willy desires.

After doing well in high school (despite childhood teasing from the popular and competitive Biff and Hap), Bernard attends college and law school, and by the end of the play, he's preparing to argue a case before the Supreme Court, even though he never mentions this to Willy.

The character of Bernard resonates in my life too. My uncle, Raymond Smith, who died at the age of eighty-six, said, "Most people don't learn or grow past the age of twenty-one." He irritated the hell out of me when he said that over and over. As a kid I took it as if all we're ever going to do is grow up, move away, marry someone, have kids, buy a car, and own a house—that simple and boring.

But my uncle was a guy who traveled the world, constantly worked in new fields, ran successful businesses, and never earned a formal education yet was hungry to learn. Global travel helped him move beyond his limited neighborhood in Camden, South Carolina, where he had grown up. He created his own classroom by living in different countries and cultures while serving in the military during World War II.

Later in life I realized that what Uncle Raymond meant to offer as a guide for me was the idea that leaving home is the just the beginning of a dangerous and exciting trip, one that will be full of *falls*. Leaving my family for the first time was a courageous act of *moving forward*. It would be a long journey, requiring that I do more than just marry and have kids and buy a car and a house. A successful career would demand curiosity that engages ongoing learning. It would create opportunities to achieve while also creating the ability to embrace those familiar *falls* that continue to arrive each day like tides on the beach.

CHAPTER 4

Moving Forward—Creating Space for Imagination

To fuel their immense bodies, giraffes consume seventy-five pounds of vegetation each day. In a neat closing of the ecological circle, their browsing stimulates new growth and thus helps propagate the very plants they consume.

—LYNN SHERR, JOURNALIST, 1997

In 1811 British textile artisans (the infamous Luddites) rose up and rebelled against economic change resulting from the Industrial Revolution. Some destroyed the high-tech looms that were triggering the loss of textile jobs. These skilled hand-loom weavers had to compete with a larger, wider, and much more productive mechanized loom—a threat so severe that on several occasions the enraged Luddites even fought against the British Army.

The Luddites weren't alone in resisting confusing change. In her 2009 *Business Week* article "Luddites of the World, Relax!" Ellen Gibson argues that there's a Western history of skepticism whenever a dramatic shift in technology occurs. Socrates dismissed writing because he said it would reduce the need to use memory. Samuel Morse, the telegraph's inventor, disliked the telephone because it offered no permanent record of conversation. And *The New York Times* blasted the expanding use of the typewriter because it shifted away from the art of "writing with one's own hand."

Similar pejoratives are tossed at today's Web, with its blogs, wikis, and expanding social media. Some criticisms of using the Web have strong validity, such as the potential to lose the skill of concentration that spurs critical and creative thinking, but when we *move forward* without fear, the courageous act signals that we'll adapt to new technology and make wise use of its offerings.

In today's post-industrial age, leadership requires much more than *falling* and *rising* and adapting to the speed of technological change. The challenging process must stimulate *a dream*, an authentic passion of where to travel next. When we choose to stand, it is more than *rising*; we're claiming ourselves—often for the first time since childhood.

Environments for Dreaming

I'm amazed that the giraffe only sleeps about thirty minutes each day with rest periods broken into six five-minute naps. The alert animal constantly grazes to discover new areas to feed because if the herd stands too long and becomes static, it risks being attacked by its main predator—the lion.

Like the giraffe, companies and employees must move forward, resting less than in past decades. That can be difficult, especially when a new technology disrupts the serene landscape we're comfortable grazing in. I've learned to appreciate the act of dreaming, a useful tool when you're dealing with significant change and a sturdy technique to keep *moving forward.*

Using our imaginations is a way to remain vibrant and keeps us from becoming too comfortable. It strengthens our guard and reduces our vulnerability so that we don't become prey to lions: a rival company, a sudden layoff, or an even greater economic collapse than we experienced in 2008 during the start of the Great Recession. Dreaming mirrors a rebirth because the act replenishes and calms. By imagining, we're participating in ongoing learning—an environment that is energizing, offers direction, and creates an urge to nurture dreams into reality.

In his 2010 article "Daydream Believer," published in *The Chronicle of Higher Education,* James Seckington cautions that our last chance to dream occurs in college before we are told to "dress for adulthood." What's misunderstood today is that you're hard at work while dreaming, a creative toil that often leads to original thoughts. Even in the second half of the information age, the act of dreaming often is considered childish or immature and displays a lack of taking responsibility in our lingering highly structured business settings. The irony is that without dreaming, this country wouldn't have pioneering ideas such as putting a man on the moon or, one day, even Mars. Dreaming helps each profession advance in an increasingly complex and intersecting global economy.

Remember the 1988 movie *Big?* Today it's ranked forty-second on the American Film Institute's "100 Years...100 Laughs" list and was listed as the tenth-best film in the fantasy genre by AFI in June 2008. *Empire* magazine also named *Big* one of the 500 greatest movies of all time.

Tom Hanks plays a thirteen-year-old kid, who early in the story gets his wish to become an adult. Trapped inside a thirty-one-year-old body, the boy finds a data entry job at a major toy company in New York City. The CEO is floored by the low-level employee's unusual creativity (pure imagination has no boundaries).

Yet by the film's conclusion, the child inside Hanks's adult body endures intense stress and burdens rooted in dated corporate structure, boundaries, and management style. Hanks loses the child within who organically dreams, along with his unrestricted imagination that generated successful ideas for the New York City toy company.

In *Still Surprised: A Memoir of a Life in Leadership,* USC professor Warren Bennis reveals that it's not just the young who are creative. Bennis rarely thinks about death or aging and works full time at the age of eighty-eight. He models his outlook after his close friend, Sam Jaffe, a Hollywood agent who died in 2000 at the age of ninety-eight and always lived in the present and the future. "The most fortunate old people," Bennis suggests, "don't lose the curiosity, energy, playfulness, and joy they had when they were young.... I take an almost childlike pleasure in each new day. There is always something new to see, to taste, to hear, to learn."

Dreaming unleashes a person's uniqueness, which is vital to company learning. If businesses today don't shape a climate for personal dreaming, they'll end up stuck in the twentieth century's traditional planning, becoming myopic and functional but not responsive to change by implementing the strongest ideas to *move forward.*

MIT's Peter Senge warns that you can't just run off to the annual planning meeting and articulate personal dreams through a forty-eight-hour weekend on a luxurious mountaintop retreat. Twenty-first-century leaders must encourage imagination as a daily ritual, making it as important as a solitary morning walk. Meetings create a veneer dream because they're coordinated and structured, with a facilitator guiding attendees through the process while notes are taken, and then everyone goes back to work. In what should be a fading model, original thinking is never fully integrated.

There's hope, however, that more companies and organizations will shift from last century's style of acting "busy" to a new environment of calmly *moving forward to feed like the giraffe*—to appreciate that the quiet dreamer should be encouraged to come up and wrestle with personal ideas before presenting them within a team where creative feedback will help shape the individual's dream into a broader vision that one day can be tested in the real-time business world.

Dreaming is moving online too.

In her book *The Game of Life and How to Play It,* American game designer Jane McGonigal says she believes developers of serious games may one day win the Nobel Peace Prize (first-rate dreaming). She views gamers (like giraffes in herds) as being "among the most collaborative people on Earth." Often disparaged as sophomoric, gaming requires intense concentration and effort and is the "best hope we have for solving the most complex problems of our time," McGonigal says.

Gamers are global, active, and connected. China has more than two hundred million of them, the US 183 million, India 105 million, Europe one hundred million, and Vietnam ten million. A growing group of organizations is convinced that serious games will provide tangible, real-world results. In fact, McGonigal's gaming research has received support from the American Heart Association, the National Academy of Sciences, and the US Department of Defense.

McGonigal stresses that we're at a tipping point; we have freedom as a culture to do something much more meaningful with gaming. We can't wreck an entire generation of optimistic, focused, and creative people who wish to play games but also hope to change the world. "Game designers need to wake up and realize that they are playing with powerful tools," McGonigal writes, "and with that power comes a responsibility to make a meaningful difference in the world."

The World Bank recently created such a game to spur imagination, which may help solve complex global problems such as hunger, disease, poverty, and lack of sustainable energy, education, and healthcare. Facebook games such as FarmVille and Mafia Wars reveal how intensely focused gamers are as they play and how connected they become with competitors, forming close ties that lead to expanding networks—the twenty-first-century new *herd*.

The World Bank's online game EVOKE was designed to empower young people to work through major problems together. The game is told through a thrilling graphic novel that's not only entertaining but also *serious*. Anyone around the globe can play. Through a series of ten online missions in ten weeks, players generate ideas to address thorny world problems. Those with the most innovative ideas are flown to Washington, DC, where they receive mentorships with experienced business leaders and social innovators, gradually moving the best dreams through the pipeline and into tangible businesses.

The Jeff Bezos Dream

In an interview with the Academy of Achievement, a museum of living history in Washington, DC, Jeff Bezos, founder and CEO of Amazon.com, Inc., recalls how he had a stable job on Wall Street with excellent pay, including a regular year-end bonus. He also had a dream, an early 1990s yearning to participate in the latest technology (the Internet) by launching a company to sell books online. When Bezos went to his director to discuss leaving the firm, the men took a two-hour stroll through Central Park. His director urged Bezos to take forty-eight hours to reflect before making a final decision about leaving the firm. He liked Bezos's entrepreneurial idea but felt the risk was better suited for someone without such an ideal job. Bezos's wife, Mackenzie, was supportive, however, encouraging her husband's risk so that he could work on a project that inspired that rare adult emotion—passion.

Within forty-eight hours, Bezos made a risky decision to keep *moving forward* to learn. What helped him act was a long-term framework that he called "regret minimization." By imagining his life ahead to the age of an octogenarian, he considered sticking with his current job instead of taking the dangerous leap to form an unpredictable start-up named Amazon.com.

By envisioning his life decades ahead, Bezos discovered that he wouldn't be disappointed about taking the risk at age eighty, but he absolutely would regret not attempting to get involved with the Internet while in his thirties. Imagination minimized his regrets, eliminating any short-term anxiety about reduced pay and the loss of his yearly holiday bonus. Bezos understood that decisions are imperfect and often fail, yet he yearned to learn more in the brisk, technology-driven 1990s.

What's remarkable is that Bezos *moved forward* like Google and Apple did, without an original economic model. The business risks were clear; Barnes and Noble, Borders, and Books-A-Million—all brick-and-mortar stores—stood in front of him blocking his path to feed. Yet here was a guy coming out of nowhere, asking the world to come buy his books. Bezos embraced a commitment to nurture his dream through to a concrete reality, risking most of his money and other resources to launch Amazon.com.

The Art of Interacting with Customers

Jeff Bezos is a giraffe of technology. He had the audacity to offer ideas that were innovative (and controversial) by openly explaining to Amazon's customers more about their buying behavior. He developed interactive capabilities that asked customers to review products and then be key players in which products they wanted and how they preferred to receive them. He never offered his customers unilateral loyalty programs, the dated corporate technique to create communities. Bezos wished to sincerely connect with customers. He's a key founder, helping to lay the framework for the dramatic rise of Web 2.0.

Amazon allowed its customers to post book reviews (feedback visible to all online) about their buying experience. Amazon deployed what Walmart knew but would not share—when a customer purchased this book or that CD, they also might buy other products. Based on users' past behavior, Amazon offered an organic learning exchange. The company knew its customers better by "listening" via technology. The genius of Web 2.0 is that there's an open, natural, and interactive dynamic between the Web host and users rather than that familiar, unilateral transaction of simply purchasing merchandise.

As a passionate user of Amazon, I've discovered that the company has learned much about me through my interacting with the company's website. Like a dear companion, the company knows the types of music, books, and merchandise I'm interested in exploring. Like a giraffe, Amazon looks out for me by frequently informing me about new music that is relevant to my broad tastes, from jazz to gospel to rock. I'm a Carlos Santana fan, and before the singer had developed his own website, Amazon had not only created a community of fans but also a single point to purchase his biographies, music, and other related Santana merchandise.

Web 1.0 was the electrification of the library, offering users the ability to find information. Web 2.0 supports a venue where each day people interact and form genuine, relevant communities. It's organic and flat—neither top-down nor hyper-controlling. If we use it wisely through selected content and limited time spent online, Web 2.0 offers a dynamic learning environment.

Amazon served as a *lookout post* for the fledgling e-commerce communities that were emerging in the 1990s. Despite cynicism and resistance, the company took risks to develop technology that sought not simply to virtualize the commercial experience of the normal bookstore. Bezos followed a dream to not only use new media to buy and sell but also to provide a higher intellectual and emotional service.

Another innovative Amazon interaction began after I had published several academic research reports. Historically, academic and professional journals had archived past issues as hard copies or on microfiche. In the 1990s they began to archive them electronically, but there was no link to the Internet for most of these archives. Amazon (and Google) led the path to the democratization of the access to these records. For most of us, accessing these past issues previously required a costly subscription, which limited our ability to use others' academic and professional journals.

I directly benefited from this quick, open access when I was selected to serve as an expert witness for a major case. A law firm performed a Google search through which they found articles and academic research (about auditing and fraud) on my CV and immediately could retrieve them for free or a nominal fee through Amazon. Initially my papers had been saved as hard copies or on floppy disks and weren't accessible on current PC platforms. Amazon made these reports available through PDFs for a download purchase, including ones from the early 1990s that hadn't yet been formally digitized.

Amazon's access provides a permanent link to a wealth of knowledge that formerly was not shared with the public and thus did not contribute to a broader learning process, the twenty-first-century *moving forward* to graze. Organizations must embrace open learning, which is predicated on its members having connection to information. Public access makes ideas more available to broader herds that can share their grazing experiences leading to new paths.

Instead of competing with Google's library initiative, Amazon adopted digital works such as mine as a means to make often-obscure information available, which benefits communities in need of this narrow-in-scope research. Amazon never acted like their territorial-based competitors Borders or Barnes and Noble, which offered a unilateral buying experience with a veneer community in their cafés. Amazon sought to develop inclusive, interactive, and organic communities in which people can share, learn, and grow.

Fighting Change Versus Moving Forward Through Innovation

Early on, Amazon adopted a giraffe-like approach that focuses on the feeding of the herds by giving customers better value and lower price instead of the old style of producing negative ads about other companies or badmouthing them. Amazon recently made the top tier of *Fortune*'s "Most Admired Companies" list. Amazon's customer service ranked higher than any other retailer's, according to a recent National Retail Federation survey. On average, the company sells their products at a rate of 6 percent less than Walmart and 9 percent less than Best Buy (the brick-and-mortar giants).

Amazon grew faster than any company in retail history. It took Walmart twenty-seven years to hit thirty billion dollars in sales while Amazon hit the mark in just sixteen years (with inflation-adjusted dollars). From 1999 to 2010, sales at Borders dropped by 44 percent to 2.3 billion dollars while Amazon's increased 808 percent to 14.9 billion dollars.

The result of fighting change? In 2011, Borders filed for bankruptcy.

Recently, the rise of digital books caused publishers to fight back against Amazon and attempt to slow Bezos down. This goal won't be easy and isn't the right tactic. If publishers don't *move forward* soon, they'll lose not only what they have but also the opportunity to build their business through Web 2.0. Today's competitive landscape doesn't offer time to adjust as it did twenty or thirty years ago.

Kindle 2 and Kindle Fire allow users to subscribe (for a fee) to newspapers and magazines without advertising. The new technology can store nearly 1,500 books. Once sold via Kindle, e-books will add revenues for publishers and authors, evidence of Bezos's argument that he wants to preserve book reading and improve it, but never replace it. He simply wants to help guide the industry to *move forward*. Electronic devices such as Kindles and iPads and others coming will facilitate e-learning, but the classroom and hardcopy will remain. It will be an age of options and choices, a boundless ability to pursue each alternative, enabled by technology. All industries must embrace this untidy yet inspiring business model if they want to grow.

Bezos continues to *feed*, as shown through Amazon's Kindle Fire (or Apple's iPad), which offers specialized apps that allow me to read *The Economist*—not the short version online but the full edition that mimics the paper copy. By paying, I'm not penalized with the scaled-down experience, and I'm also not cutting down trees. The digital subscription service takes the old experience and delivers it to me in a fresh way, resurrecting the magazine and newspaper business through subscriptions delivered to Kindle and iPad rather than my door.

Amazon (as well as companies such as Apple and Google) is changing the publishing world through *wild* innovation. It isn't all pretty, but you can no longer debate the significant change that is happening and is increasingly influenced by artificial intelligence. We are living in a Jetson-inspired era, but it's not a silly cartoon. Like Bezos, publishers must respect customers and ask for their input, creating an active community around their products. Bezos has helped change centuries of behavior and is akin to other inventors, from Alexander Graham Bell to Thomas Edison. In the Bloomberg.com article "Amazon's Bezos Fuels Tablet Wars with $199 Kindle," Nancy F. Koehn, a professor of business administration at Harvard Business School, says, "Amazon is such a smart learning organization. It's like a biological organism that through natural selection and adaptation just keeps learning and growing."

Bezos's act to move the book-selling business down a new path is important not only for his world but also ours. E-commerce is a vital element of our economy. One day historians may view Jeff

Bezos as the Thomas Jefferson of e-commerce because he helped to revolutionize the way the economy operates. After World War II, companies dictated consumer behavior, but today consumers are dictating company behavior through blogs, wikis, Facebook, Twitter, and other growing social media that will continue to arrive. Customers are expressing their interests and demanding how and what they purchase. Amazon created some of the key technology to support these twenty-first-century interactions, and validated this business model's economic value through its ongoing success—50 percent growth in quarterly revenues and sales that may approach 50 billion dollars or more in 2012.

The old bookstores are struggling as they fell behind with their version of e-commerce that simply put their store on the Web rather than creating organic communities where customers played key roles. Through the supply chain of authors, publishers, artists, and vendors, Bezos has made a declaration of e-commerce, stating that modern consumers are free to decide, contribute, and purchase in any manner they wish. It's been one of the biggest shifts in the publishing industry since Johannes Gutenberg introduced printing about six hundred years ago. "The only really necessary people in the publishing process now are the writer and reader. Everyone who stands between those two has both risk and opportunity," states Amazon executive Russell Grandinetti in David Streitfield's *New York Times* article "Amazon Signs Up Authors, Writing Publishers Out of Deal."

The US is beginning to adapt to flattening technology. We're talking about changing century-old habits and behavior. It's impossible to shift from brick-and-mortar to point-and-click overnight, yet we can't fight the transition like the music industry did through the late 1990s and early 2000s when Napster and file sharing began to erode the music industry's business model. We must adopt technology, wrestle with it, discover how it works best in our lives, and learn how it helps businesses and customers, government and nonprofits, public schools and higher education (broader communities) to become smarter and more productive. With that dream and value in mind, technology supports rather than destroys, guiding all of us to *move forward* and *graze*.

Bezos doesn't view mobile gadgets as simple hardware. "We don't think of the Kindle Fire as a tablet," he says in the article "Amazon's Bezos Fuels Tablet Wars with $199 Kindle" on Bloomberg.com. "We think of it as a service."

Moving Forward Through Project-Based Careers

Over the years, three to five jobs per lifetime has shifted to ten to fourteen career experiences. For my generation, the goal was to leave college and find serious work at one major company. Teachers stayed with the same school district or school for thirty-five years. Once tenured, professors stopped sending out CVs. Sports superstars such as Cal Ripkin, Bill Russell, Willis Reed, and Jerry West remained loyal to a single team through their lengthy careers. Most futurists today, however, predict that professionals must develop a mosaic of work experiences to achieve in their careers.

Our new century will require that companies and employees have common goals of gathering information and seeking new experiences by pursuing growth that follows a zigzagging, often confusing path. My grandmother faced change approximately every thirty years, but today you can't delay adapting for decades. You won't be part of a community. You won't excel professionally if you don't embrace technology for learning.

Stan Davis and Christopher Meyer, authors of the book *Blur: The Speed of Change in the Connected Economy,* highlight that "increasingly, value resides in information and relationships—things you can't see at all and often can't measure." In this new "blurring" economy, most of us eventually will be "free agents," and how we spend our attention and emotion will have a greater impact on our lives. Networking will be more important. Learning how to manage our "own stock price" will be an added responsibility, and work will be much more than simply making money. According to Davis and Meyer, free agents—enabled by technology—seek to work for companies with "enabling infrastructure, better access to people you want in your network...more flexibility in work scheduling, more creative work content."

As we *move forward* over the next ninety years, most of us will be our own agents. The one-job-for-life career will fade. We won't have the union-based, clear structure and security—no single model anymore. Unions are no different from corporations. Most failed to help their members embrace change to grow rather than become static in their careers. It'll be tough, but we won't *move forward* by resistance, only through flexibility.

During the 1980s, if you switched jobs every two or three years as I did, you were stereotyped as unstable, opportunistic, or just plain odd. When I interviewed at Bristol-Myers for an internal auditing position, I'd had several positions already, starting with Arthur Anderson, Geosource Controls, Sonate/El Paso, and US Home. My aim was to gain experience in a new market. I had worked in the oil and gas business in the Middle East and parts of South America and the North Sea, but I wanted to switch to customer products to broaden my experience. I took risks to *move forward* in the 1980s when the idea of frequently changing jobs was verboten.

During my interview at Bristol-Myers, a distinguished British gentleman said, "Hubert, my boy, you have an outlandishly dismal record. You need to gain control of your career and stabilize it. You're opportunistic, bounce around, and seem a bit unstable. You need to put your career on track. Find an organization for life and follow the tradition that has always led to success, commitment, and loyalty to one entity. You need to grasp the rules of the game, or you'll never accomplish anything."

He was right, because his argument was exactly the feeling back then. He, and others, decided that you should stay somewhere for ten, fifteen, even thirty years, but I responded to him, "You're right, sir. I don't have the normal five to ten years at this corporation or that nonprofit or government agency, but I know more than people who sit at one job and become static, failing to learn as decades pass."

Because of well-researched and selected job shifts, I've worked in large and small operations, from corporate to manufacturing to managing out in the field by traveling around our planet. My interviewer at Bristol-Myers couldn't see the value in it. By that time I had earned my MBA, CMA, and CPA, but he viewed me as an unstable force, not a contributor. He needed me in one place, that neat and tidy box he had to check on his form.

He was focused on a dated paradigm, last century's lifelong employment model. It was acceptable to work in public accounting and then shift to corporate industry, but then you must stay for life as though serving a prison term. No back and forth, but rather driving down the linear highway until you reach your professional grave.

More similar to the twenty-first-century "free agent" model, I envisioned my career as a set of eclectic experiences that included internal auditing, public accounting, and global travel. When I met with my friend Robert Carter in the 1980s, he convinced me to join his private company with a focus on consulting—a giraffe-inspired, zigzagging path to discover a hidden grove of acacia trees.

Leaving the comfort of a well-paying and respected corporate job to work in an unproven business was risky. Through consulting, however, I found new opportunities, and the work prepared and inspired me for my doctorial program. Once a serious clock watcher, through consulting I became engaged. I was no longer a corporate soldier but a field general thrust into the complexities of battle.

Robert was that rare leader who embraced mosaic careers. With Robert, I didn't have to lie about my dream to earn a PhD. Years later, when I came back to work with him, we doubled the size of his company Easi, Inc. Robert was a giraffe-inspired leader, embracing a style that wasn't in vogue at the time. He created an authentic learning environment for me to gain skills to be even more successful and to keep *moving forward*, even if that meant leaving his company for academia.

At most other firms, I had to create the impression that I would stay at a company for a decade. Each time I changed jobs, I took risks to *move forward* because I had to start over to some extent; I was that "new kid on the block." I realized that to be an effective academician, I needed to learn more about the broader business environment. I treated my jobs as rotational internships, gaining exposure from research in the field and bringing that knowledge to the classroom.

In the CNN.com article "Why America Is Going the Way of the Freelancer," Gene Zaino, who serves on the expert advisory board of the Human Capital Institute, states that businesses must become increasingly agile to compete in a global economy of frequent change. Businesses are moving to a "project world" in which companies can "buy things in packages—small units." Consultants, independent contractors, and freelancers will be more in demand. Social media enables freelancers and consultants to learn about projects and allows project leaders to learn about them. Due to frequent change in our global economy, Zaino predicts the project-based workforce will grow in value during the twenty-first century.

If you came to my organization today and had an eclectic background, I'd view it as a benefit to my firm and leverage your experience in the age of Web 2.0. I keep strong relationships with employee alumni, encouraging them to *move forward*, knowing there's a good chance we'll connect again. It's the notion of serendipity, the boomerang that soars far away before it unexpectedly returns. Companies will create that boomerang effect by encouraging mosaic or project-based experiences in which individuals risk moving far away only to return one day with stronger credentials and more innovative thinking.

The traditional model of hiring isn't changing quickly enough. We need to admire people because of their mosaic experiences within their field that reveal their breadth and depth. Length of service with a single firm once symbolized loyalty but today may highlight an inability to take risks that lead to learning, growth, and creative contribution.

Freedom Defined in the Twenty-First Century

Today's technology is bringing freedom to our shrinking planet. Thomas Friedman highlighted the trend in his book *The World Is Flat*. It's always been a universal truth from the hammer to the Gutenburg press, yet today it's affecting more humans than ever before. In 1969, poet William Stafford wrote about the importance of this frequently used abstraction that we use casually and rarely define through a unique angle. Stafford, however, defines the vague umbrella term of "freedom" as something that could benefit all.

Freedom

Freedom is not following a river
Freedom is following a river,
though, if you want to.
It is deciding now by what happens now.
It is knowing that luck makes a difference.

No leader is free; no follower is free—
the rest of us can often be free.
Most of the world are living by
creeds too odd, chancy, and habit-forming
to be worth arguing about by reason.

If you are oppressed, wake up about
four in the morning; most places
you can usually be free some of the time
if you wake up before other people.

Being able to make a *decision* is the essence of "freedom." Stafford suggests that if you literally "wake up about four in the morning…before other people," you'll have some room to be free.

Does freedom require "enough space" so that we can be ourselves, so that we can dream and be original and creative, optimistic, and productive?

Does "wake up" also mean that we wake up our attitudes, so that we're not simply *following* a river selected by the traditional CEO or manager but rather *choosing* to follow a certain river?

Last century, most leaders made independent decisions, but were they actually limited and constrained by a business model designed to ensure the loyalty of *followers* and the success of the leader's policies?

As Jeff Bezos did with Amazon, we must break the industrial-age model in which "No leader is free; no follower is free" because both the leader and follower *follow* that powerfully flowing, one-direction river, rather than *choosing* to follow a river *if they want to.*

To encourage individuals to dream and continually *move forward*, leaders must create genuine environments where people don't have to "wake up about four in the morning" to be independent, self-reliant, and make decisions. They need daily work settings that encourage them to be un-swayed by the attitudes, expectations, or edicts of others. We need enough space so that each day leads us to imagine controversial, quirky, and unique ideas like those at Google, Amazon, and Apple—innovations that are changing not only business but also the planet.

Stafford may be stating that to be truly free we must not become prisoners of trends, group think, ideology, or tradition. Instead leaders today must encourage employees to question, to trust their ideas, and to continue to grow if they are truly free, which requires twenty-first-century *choice*, not twentieth-century *following.*

CHAPTER 5

The Lions of Change Destroy Creative Settings

Under direct threat of attack, a giraffe generally beats a hasty retreat, although a female shepherding a small baby will stand her ground. Giraffes never employ their knobby horns against predators, but they can deliver a crushing blow with the hind foot, chop-kick with the forefoot like a horse, or strike with the whole stiff foreleg.

—J. BRISTOL FOSTER, BIOLOGIST, 1977

The Tragedy of Failing to Spot Lions

Anne Parmenter, head coach of Trinity College's women's field hockey team, is a mountaineering guide and graduate of the National Outdoor Leadership School. She's scaled the peaks of the world's highest mountains, including Denali, Aconcagua, and Mount Blanc. When she attempted to reach the summit of Mount

Everest in 2004, joining a quickly organized team, she witnessed the *lion*-inspired traits of bullying, direct threats, and stolen gear.

It's odd that when the tallest herbivore spots its main predator in the distance, the giraffe moves toward the lion, never away. The giraffe isn't violent the moment there's conflict, and so who's most vulnerable, the growling carnivore or the calm herbivore? The emotional fighter or the focused observer?

The giraffe has a clear view of the lion stalking, preparing to attack. The giraffe protects itself by deciding how to navigate the danger so as to keep *moving forward* on a clear pathway to feed.

It's never easy to spot *lions*, especially in our growing "free agent" professional lives where many of us engage in mosaic careers, quarterly consulting, and project work that will expose us to vast numbers of people through intense interaction—similar to the environment Anne Parmenter suddenly found herself in on the slopes of Mount Everest.

In these twenty-first-century professional settings, we often fail to notice *lions* (leaders or colleagues) as dangerous predators. We admire and rely on their resumes and traits that highlight graduation from a competent MBA program, a high IQ, or an aggressive, hierarchical management style.

But we know that lions have a violent goal—*to hide, stalk, and kill.*

When the *lions'* traits of bullying and threats take hold, organizations collapse.

In her *Washington Post* article "A Leadership Nightmare Turned Everest Triumph," Anne Parmenter writes that she abandoned the slope at 21,500 feet because there wasn't a smidgen of honest teamwork established and the setting grew more dangerous each day. She headed down the mountain because the lions had destroyed trust.

The ugly reality is that we all face lions, even with giraffe-inspired leadership. It's not easy to know when to avoid danger, stand firm, or execute that lethal kick like giraffes do in the wild. Few of us respond with calm to the lion's attack. But these real-world emotional conflicts—and our responses to them—are often the most important learning opportunities throughout a forty-year career.

Parmenter returned to the US dispirited after her encounter with lions that blocked her path to the summit of Mount Everest. For two years she reflected on the unsuccessful climb, thinking about the nature of the attack and how she might have responded.

In 2006 she flew back to Tibet keenly aware that lion-inspired behavior exists, even in a passionate sport such as mountain climbing. Before her second expedition, Parmenter spent time researching (similar to giraffes moving toward—never away from—the lion crouching in the distance) before she discovered an outfitter who worked with her to find a team of climbers with similar needs. She writes:

> *I was fortunate to rewrite my Everest nightmare, summiting on May 25th with a small group of wonderful people. With cooperation, teamwork, and a little luck, we spent forty-five minutes on the summit together—with blue-bird skies, no wind, and a view of the world that remains etched in my memory today.*

Lions crouching in dense African brush aren't easy to spot, even for the vertically gifted giraffe. In today's business settings, lions continue to hide, shatter teams, and destroy learning environments—twentieth-century behavior that limits twenty-first-century company innovation.

After both journeys, Parmenter realized that leadership and teamwork mattered as much as her decades of mountaineering experience. Giraffe-inspired skills of "competence, tolerance for adversity and uncertainty, communication, and self-awareness" guided her team to the summit. And this style must guide US business through the twenty-first century to keep our country *moving forward.*

The Lions of Change

When the giraffe spots an area where it can guide the herd to foliage and protection, the herd calmly moves forward, although occasionally a lion appears, blocking the path to the feeding ground.

The giraffe must make a life-or-death decision.

Often it walks away or gives warnings but rarely launches that crushing blow, though the threat of the giraffe's lethal kick is known to the lion. In some specific way, giraffes always deal with lions so they can move forward to graze, the herbivore's daily goal.

Standing up to lions is as tricky in the professional world as it is in the wild. We're stopped and yanked off the path of *moving forward.* We're thrust backward into the primitive mode of "survive or die." In work settings few of us stand up to the lion with as much ease and focus as giraffes do in nature. But to make use of the encounter, we must commit to the goal of feeding (learning). If that's our genuine focus, we'll have more skills at negotiating these conflicts when the next lion blocks our path to growth.

A key aspect to moving forward is to focus on the *herd.* If we keep that audience—not our individual egos—as our guide, we'll attempt to make the proper decisions and achieve better results. Indra Nooyi is such a giraffe-inspired leader who had to face lions blocking her path—the *lions of change.*

After she became the CEO of PepsiCo, Nooyi launched "Performance with Purpose," a new business model that "focuses on delivering sustainable growth by investing in a healthier future for people and the planet" as reported in Chrystal Houston's 2010 article "Duty of Care," which appeared in Mays Business Online.

Nooyi initiated significant change away from the unhealthy twentieth-century model to a smarter twenty-first-century pathway by suggesting the removal all of the company's sugary drinks from schools around the world by 2012; the reduction of salt in the company's biggest brands by 25 percent by 2015; and the reduction of saturated fat by 15 percent in its snacks by 2020. She shifted from "fun for you" products (chips and sugared soft drinks) to "better for you" products (popcorn, baked chips, and zero-calorie drinks) and "good for you" products (granola bars and fruit juices).

PepsiCo's healthier approach led Nooyi to face numerous lions, also known as skeptics. Many attacked her by questioning her sincerity—was this simply another PepsiCo PR tactic recycled through a "healthy" brand? Nooyi, however, stood up to the *lions of change* through maintaining a clear goal, warning the company not to take the dead-end route like the tobacco industry had.

Firms are now being held legally responsible for health problems and penalized accordingly. Nooyi imagined the company moving beyond the familiar idea of "just beating Coke." Unlike the tobacco industry, which produces cigarettes that are linked to cancer, Nooyi is leading PepsiCo and the soft drink and snack industry to find solutions for obesity and related health problems that her company's products are being linked to in the US. She doesn't want PepsiCo to mirror the tobacco industry, which fought change, lost, and then moved overseas where they don't have to grow their tobacco in some particular way and continue to ruin the health of others.

Nooyi was firm with the *lions of change*, arguing that PepsiCo's focus must be on people's health throughout the next century. She hired experts for PepsiCo's research and development teams to guide the company to offer healthier products that earn ten billion dollars today, which will only grow in the next decade to reach thirty billion dollars of PepsiCo's assets. Nooyi stood up to the *lions of change* with a belief that argued that we can't run away to foreign countries in the twenty-first century because that's not the kind of change that leads to long-term growth. "Performance with Purpose" isn't a surface deal for her. Nooyi is honest and accountable and has a global background that provides an awareness and understanding of others. She embraces a variety of input, which is key to standing firm when the ubiquitous lions block the path to company innovation.

The Twenty-First-Century Giraffe Kick— Continual Learning

What the hell is *creative tension?*

MIT's Peter Senge describes the paradoxical term as a vital environment in which an employee can share his or her dreams with colleagues. But more important in the twenty-first century is *how* these dreams are shared. Today *dialogue* is as essential as *discussion*, but few CEOs and companies actually know or care about the stark differences.

Dialogue is trickier to inspire than *discussion* because it requires genuine openness, critical listening (rather than ignoring what you don't wish to hear), and patient reflection. In true dialogue, no decisions are made. There are no winners or losers. It's a magical setting (mirroring the young boy in the movie *Big*), where one person can share an imperfect yet authentic dream, and others are free to offer reactions that build on the idea rather than rip it apart through industrial-age competitiveness.

That's an aspect of *creative tension.*

"Tension" shouldn't connote twentieth-century anger through emotional office explosions. And that's exactly what's difficult to establish—unemotional listening coupled with patient reflection to guide an idea through "creative tension" and on to an authentically shared idea, team intelligence, often improving it from the individual's dream that sparked the imaginative process.

On the contrary, in a typical *discussion,* we make a decision about whether to launch the idea into the real world. There are distinct winners and losers. But there's no genuine *dialogue* (routinely dismissed as children's bedtime fantasy hour with dear Mommy), and that rejection is a twenty-first-century storm that's moving closer to our shores.

In his 2011 *Harvard Business Review* article "Hold Conversations, Not Meetings," Tony Golsby-Smith, CEO of 2nd Road in Australia, extends the term "dialogue" to mean *conversations* in which people (most often outside of the workplace) easily chat with an openness that promotes a full range of thinking and stimulates "creative, right-brain intelligence in people."

Conversations help us explore complicated, messy circumstances for which we don't know the outcome. Golsby-Smith sees "discussions" as *meetings* where real issues aren't fully addressed because meetings stifle imagination and encourage ubiquitous nitpicking, prompting most of us sitting at the conference table to censor ourselves, disengage, and lose sight of the bigger picture.

And last century's model of communication risks failure today.

Companies and organizations need more conversations such as those encouraged by Whole Foods, so that unique ideas get nurtured and progress to original team thinking that sparks innovative action. Conversations are energizing, nonthreatening, and consensus building—a democracy of the best ideas that have value for others, not simply the company.

Throughout its thirty years in the food business, Whole Foods continues to stimulate such an environment because it's rooted in the company motto "Whole Foods, Whole People, Whole Planet." The company contributes at least 5 percent of its after-tax profits to charities, pays employees their regular salary to participate in community charity events such as running in a race for breast cancer, and constantly seeks creative ideas from all levels of staff; the company reaches out to employees to help discover their individual dreams.

"I've made a valuable contribution to Whole Foods," says John Mackey, the company's founder, in the 2010 *Austin American-Statesman* article "At Whole Foods, Team Management Goes All the Way to the Top" by Brian Gaar. "But so have thousands of other people. That's one of our secrets...the fact that we do really have a team approach to the organization, an empowerment approach."

The company's giraffe-inspired, herd-focused leadership (still too rare in corporate America) mirrors its culture that prefers sharing ideas through teams, not through individual egos, which guides Whole Foods to emerge swiftly from the Great Recession.

I recently served NASA at various facilities throughout the United States. There's a famous 1960s story of shared ideas being conveyed during a visit by President Johnson to the NASA facility named after him in Houston, Texas. As Johnson was walking down the hall, he was greeted by one of the staff, and the president asked the man what he did.

"I'm helping to put a man on the moon," the man replied.

Apparently, when Johnson learned that the man was in fact a custodian, he was so pleased by the man's response that he continued to lobby aggressively for the space program throughout his administration. This is a powerful example of engagement through a shared dream. This occurred prior to email, the five-thousand-day-old Web, social media, and even the publication of some of the more progressive management and leadership books.

Even the lowest members on the 1960s organizational rung embraced roles in something much broader them themselves. The janitor's response to the President of the United States was honest, accurate, and team focused. Clean facilities created an environment that stimulated an effective execution of the scientific and engineering professional roles and led to the successful launch of space missions for more than a decade.

Leadership in the second half of the information age must inspire passionate learning settings at all levels of a company. If leaders encourage dreaming, dialogue, and reflection, they earn (not order) employee engagement because people truly feel empowered by lifelong learning and growth. Trust spreads. And those frequent defense mechanisms revealed through emotional politics and game playing slip away as dreams *move forward* to tangible ideas that will enter a business reality.

Emotional Tension Nourishes Only the Lion

Most of us aren't trained for, respect, or even understand our roles in this growing twenty-first-century creative setting. Genuine listening and reflective openness of a colleague's idea help guide it forward to a shared vision—often improving the individual's dream, the wonderful spark.

Most leadership today isn't genuinely fostering conversations. More often, a veneer dialogue is set forth through phony openness because decisions have been made, strong beliefs and values are locked, and the familiar emotional conflict ensues—a highlight of the July 2011 congressional debt-ceiling fight.

Emotional (not *creative*) tension dominates most of our workplaces, and people instinctively pull out of the setting, splintering off into group think (not *shared vision*)—a pattern that not only destroys any chance of real conversations but also takes the individual's dream and reduces its quality. Today's group think (what

MIT's Peter Senge calls a "learning disability") is often less intelligent and successful than the individual's original dream.

Companies were fine operating this way in the last century because the pace of change was slower and weak ideas could be adjusted for over time. But this isn't the case in our rushed, complex new century, a period in which we need more dreamers generating stronger ideas that continue to enter the company's innovative pipeline.

Senge observed that a jazz band could execute different rhythms and beats that by logic should sound cacophonous but with the right team of musicians would transform individual talents into a broader, more complex sound that melodiously blends, creating something fresh, beyond conventional, and more attractive than the familiar.

Think back to that youthful sports team, elementary school drama club, or Scout troop like Bill Cosby's experience in this book's foreword. Remember those settings where disparate personalities worked together to miraculously increase the talent level to win a championship or prize or recognition. Remember Michael Jordon and the Chicago Bulls' six NBA championships—three in a row and then another three in a row. Or the Boston Celtics' Bill Russell, who earned eleven championships in thirteen years as a professional basketball player—an achievement unheard of in the past decade.

Why have these wonderful *herd*-like experiences become so rare today?

Google pays its employees to take one-fifth of their weekly schedule to dream, research, and reflect on something they enjoy. Freedom inspires passion for originality because there are no rules, or rivers, to follow. This 20 percent of time generates fresh ideas for the company to consider acting upon. Failure is part of the process. Google offers this creative time before that "yes" or "no" meeting takes place.

Google stimulates daily dreaming (just like the Stanford research lab does nearby) so that the best ideas continuously enter the corporate pipeline and eventually move into an unpredictable global marketplace. Google's senior engineering director,

Patrick Copeland, understands that an environment of creative tension helps the company "build the right it versus build it right." Building the right "it" is twenty-first-century innovation. It means building products or creating services that require more than an individual's dream but rather a shared dream that continues to develop before entering our blurring marketplace.

Google's concept one-fifth creative time (and that's increasing) offers tremendous benefits for companies because twenty-first-century learning kicks the *lions of creativity*. Individual, team, and company learning reduce the deadly drop-off into *emotional tension* that triggers the defense mechanisms we've all participated in. The spark from learning discourages the *lions of shared vision*, who prefer polarization, politics, and game playing.

Remember that lions want it one way—their way. Lions rigorously battle others' ideas because it's the swiftest way to block the path of significant change. But when a giraffe-inspired leader launches that lethal kick, he or she will knock that emotional lion off the pathway, providing an atmosphere for ongoing learning that promotes growth and benefits the customer, employee, and company—even the planet.

As a child in India, PepsiCo CEO Indra Nooyi "saw firsthand how corporations could harm a community, robbing it of resources and leaving ruin in its wake. 'It doesn't have to be this way,' she thought," as reported in Chrystal Houston's article "Duty of Care," which appeared in Mays Business Online.

In the past, companies believed that being socially responsible meant donating money to various charities or nonprofits in areas of natural disasters, the environment, and even green marketing. But Nooyi understands that sustainability is winning in sectors of corporate America that have embraced the growing motto "Saving the planet can save big bucks."

"Smart CEOs are investing in a more rigorous approach to the environment," adds Daniel C. Esty, an environmental policy professor at Yale Law School in the 2011 *Business Week* article "Why Sustainability is Winning Over CEOs."

Nooyi's "Performance with Purpose" highlights this leadership approach through its Walker plant in Leicester, England, the

LAY's chips of Europe. Nooyi embraced the art of having a *conversation* "with academics and outside engineers...to build a contraption that will attach to rooftop exhaust stacks, [recycling] 80 percent or more of it as water to the plant." The UK plant will use the recycled water to wash potatoes and equipment and irrigate shrubs outside, which could save one million dollars a year. The plant uses 185 million gallons of water each year, and through a major shift by embracing innovative technology, PepsiCo hopes by the end of 2013 to remove the plant from the public water grid and pull four more plants off it by 2018.

Through Nooyi's innovative efforts rooted in *conversation* with a broader *herd*—PepsiCo's Frito-Lay unit—the world's seventh-largest private delivery fleet has added 176 all-electric box trucks in California, Texas, and the Pacific Northwest, which may cut diesel consumption by half-a-million gallons a year and reduce greenhouse emission by 75 percent. The new trucks will reduce annual maintenance costs by approximately seven hundred thousand dollars.

PepsiCo's dream, which is quickly moving into reality, understands the twenty-first-century link between sustainable business practices and enormous company savings. Once dismissed as silly for business or used only as charity to generate a more "feeling" brand, sustainable business has emerged as a way for companies to respect the environment while saving money—the company's twenty-first-century *move forward* rather than the twentieth-century strategy of remaining static.

The Lion Within—Preventing Dreams from Moving to Reality

The paradox is that we all have a lion growling within us, a trait that has the potential to destroy our much needed participation in the art of dialogue, creative tension, and patient reflection. The lion within is negative, an obstacle to authentic imagination. The lion within is like a New Year's resolution, "I'm going to lose weight, exercise more, stop smoking, or go to bed earlier." The focus is on turning around something negative. Few adults have that childlike, laser focus on the optimistic—"I'm going to create something new and enjoy the time I spend working on it."

Unlike last century's charismatic leaders, today's leaders must listen more and encourage conversational environments where original ideas continually move into reality. When emotional tension dominates a work setting, people quickly abandon their dreams. They become afraid to talk and to share ideas through conversations. Conformity begins. Anxiety, stress, sadness, and worry dominate. Leaders today must engage others by clearly stating that "I'm listening, and I'm going to offer constructive rather than negative feedback," a style that leads to engagement and an improved shared vision.

Twenty-first-century leaders must earn an advanced degree in the art of conversation that stimulates learning, a key criterion to move original thinking through a messy twenty-first-century reality, as Google is attempting with librarians, educators, medical researchers, and the scientific community.

Lions will always strive to block pathways forward, but their attacks will dwindle in the twenty-first century when they attempt to stalk in authentic learning environments such as Google, Whole Foods, or PepsiCo.

Change Ain't Easy Because Lions Win in the Short Term

During the Great Depression, when poet Maya Angelou was just ten (her name at the time was Marguerite Johnson), she lived with her grandmother in Stamps, Arkansas, where her "finishing school" was a white woman's kitchen.

The cook, Miss Glory, trained Marguerite, and together they served Mrs. Viola Cullinan. At first Marguerite felt sorry for the old woman, who was homely, couldn't bear children, and had married beneath her. Gossip circulating in town hinted that Mrs. Cullinan's husband had two illegitimate children who happened to be half black. So when Mrs. Cullinan couldn't pronounce Marguerite's name, preferring "Margaret," she forgave the fading woman. For weeks she worked long hours, feeling empathy for her employer because of her barrenness and her philandering husband.

One evening, however, as Marguerite went to serve Mrs. Cullinan and her friends who had gathered on the porch, Mrs. Cullinan explained that her new hire was "usually quiet as a little mouse. Aren't you, Margaret?"

"Well, that may be," one of Mrs. Cullinan's friends interrupted, "but the name's too long. I'd never bother myself. I'd call her Mary if I was you."

Marguerite stood fuming and recognized, as if a wave had crashed over her head, the subtle racism that had replaced the overt racism she'd often heard her parents and grandparents describe.

Soon Miss Glory shared that she too had had her named changed from "Hallelujah" to "Glory" twenty years earlier, when as a young girl she was hired to work for the Cullinan family.

It was a roaring, lion-inspired environment, one that Marguerite knew she'd never repeat.

In an act of courage beyond her ten years, Marguerite stood up to the *lions of change* by devising a plan to get fired. In the Southern milieu of the 1930s, she couldn't just quit. It would bring shame to her grandmother, who owned a successful general store, so she came up with a plan. She deliberately broke one of Mrs. Cullinan's favorite china dishes, a casserole shaped like a fish, passed down through the Southern aristocratic Cullinan family, just like their racial bigotry.

At her "finishing school," Marguerite didn't learn Southern social etiquette, how to play the piano, or how to speak French. She learned to spot rituals of racial disrespect (*lions of change*) and to challenge them firmly, before launching that giraffe's rare and lethal kick. She learned that language matters and who selects your name is a mighty act. Marguerite rejected the centuries-old setting of allowing her mistress to call her "Mary," the way Hallelujah had accepted "Miss Glory."

After Marguerite stood firm and broke Ms. Cullinan's china so she could get fired, the *lions of change* fought back, and the subtle racism of name-changing instantly shifted to the overt racism of the Southern past.

"That clumsy nigger. Clumsy little black nigger," Mrs. Cullinan cried out.

Now, many decades after that childhood incident (one that Maya Angelou describes in her autobiography *I Know Why the Caged Bird Sings*), when every person Maya knew had "a hellish horror of being called out of his name," we all must stand up to the *lions of change.*

Remember that *lions* have one goal—to yank us off the path of *moving forward.*

We're thrust backward into the primitive mode of "survive or die." But to make use of the encounter, we must commit to the goal of feeding (twenty-first-century learning). If that's the genuine focus, we'll have more skills at negotiating these emotional conflicts when the next lion blocks our path to continuous growth.

After Mayo Angelou "kicked" her Southern mistress—a devoted member of the *lions of racial change*—the poet was never again prevented from *moving forward.* At the age of eighty-three, she's been nominated for the Pulitzer Prize, the National Book Award, a Tony Award, and three Grammys. She has served on two presidential committees, was awarded the National Medal of Arts, the Lincoln Medal, more than thirty honorary degrees, and the Presidential Medal of Freedom in 2011—an astonishing resume developed over seventy years because as a child she had the giraffe-inspired instinct to face the *lions of change* that attempted to block her path.

CHAPTER 6

New Herds—Blending into Diverse Communities

Giraffes move in and out of herds, forming and reforming into diverse groups without fighting, without interruption of their life-sustaining grazing on the open plains of Africa. Unlike other animals (including humans), Giraffes exist without a dominant, ongoing single leader; yet when there's a need for a leader to rise and send out warning signs, the herd accepts any member to risk the momentary role.

—DR. HUBERT GLOVER, 2012

No More Priesthoods, Fiefdoms, or Kingdoms

By nature giraffes welcome other herbivores into the herd (including zebras, wildebeests, hartebeests, and birds), animals that aren't blessed with the giraffe's extraordinary height and vision. By constantly *moving forward* to feed while living in a diverse, ever-shifting, and dangerous world, giraffes symbolize twenty-first-century leadership that centers on people working together on an increasingly level playing field.

Last century's communication technology (the telephone, radio, and television) allowed us to speak out, and we accomplished ambitious goals such as putting a man on the moon because Americans united to achieve a specific goal. Our country always has had deep divisions, yet during the Great Depression, World War II, and the Cold War, the majority of people rose to overcome these familiar fragmentations and achieved success by blending into *new herds*, taking advantage of the country's unique talent. But that past is reversing, as our once herd-inspired majority, who dealt with challenging problems last century, has shifted. We've grown comfortable, become static and solitary, losing interest in achieving cutting-edge goals that include more than a single culture or country, company or CEO.

As the giraffes of technology predicted about the hyper-paced, messy direction of our future economy, we can't simply return to the moon this century. Repetition won't work. We must *move forward* together, determined to understand the global economy, a complex yet promising setting in which the advent of technology causes geographical and socioeconomic barriers to collapse and creates a more democratic existence as well as the ability to connect to information and others.

Information is powerful.

Knowledge always has been a premium commodity, due to difficult access, but with the expanding Internet, someday the child who leads a meager existence in the developing world will have access to the same information as the child who lives in the cushy developed world. Stanford University recently offered three online computer science classes, including "Introduction to Artificial Intelligence." Two hundred thousand people from around the globe quickly signed up for these free public courses. Seven more courses will be offered in 2012 because many more professors are investing in making knowledge available to the masses, even if the masses can't pay. Students don't earn Stanford credits, but they receive vital information (once impossible for the poor to access) as well as a certificate of completion.

In the future, companies in developed countries will no longer have an automatic advantage over developing countries in the fields of education and information. It's becoming increasingly vital to leverage technology such as the Web and social media to connect with *new herds*, people who represent communities of opportunity, knowledge, and support. If we don't accept these new communities—and the information they offer us—the velocity of change will leave us ignorant in the growing knowledge age.

Since the early 1990s, we have seen the *rise* and *fall* of many giants, such as Blockbuster, Circuit City, Yahoo, AOL, and Research in Motion (RIM), the maker of BlackBerry. Who's next, Netflix? Unless we sincerely stay connected to people and share information about how the world is changing, many more organizations will struggle and fail.

Philip Kotler, S.C. Johnson & Son professor of international marketing at the Kellogg School of Management at Northwestern University, suggests a fresh *business herd* is needed in 2012— *Marketing 3.0*. We need to move past the dreary marketing archetype that told companies they "need to maximize profits and please shareholders above all else, that customers…are informed by sellers, not other customers, about purchases," as reported in Chrystal Houston's 2010 article "Marketing 3.0: Expert Discusses Paradigm Shift and the Now of Marketing," which appeared in Mays Business Online.

Unlike last century's manipulative approach, which many in the marketing community still praise, Kotler suggests that the twenty-first-century style requires authentic "connection and co-creation" with consumers. Leaders must strive to be elite listeners of others (regardless of their rank or title) and engage diverse communities in ongoing learning.

Cutting-edge technology and the rapid change that follows have shifted the industrial-age power over the customer into a new relationship. "Consumers now demand two-way communication and input into the product and services they consume," Kotler argues. "It's a dialogue, not a monologue."

Over the next decade, companies will shift further from Marketing 2.0 (listening to customers to gain insight) to Marketing 3.0 (engaging customers as co-creators of products). Businesses must sincerely commit to community building, not yesterday's brand building. In the 1950s it was a monologue from the massive brand to the tiny customer. Today we must have a broader conversation through blogs and social media so that as we create products and services we continually engage with customers' feedback, ideas, and needs.

Unfortunately that's not what's happening in the first decade of the twenty-first century.

We're still static, terrified of change, struggling as though we're standing thigh deep in quicksand, unable to move away from the twentieth-century business model that triggers those dominating nouns: "priesthoods," "fiefdoms," and "kingdoms."

Philip Kotler understands that we're entering a *new-herd* century in which "humanity is moving into an age of creativity, where reliance on muscles is giving way to reliance on brainpower. Customers are not only looking for products and services that satisfy their needs but also searching for experiences and business models that touch their human spirit."

Open Leadership—Customers Embrace the Role of the New CEO

In October 2009, former Yale English professor William Deresiewicz delivered a lecture to the plebe class at the United States Military Academy at West Point. His call for a new military leadership grabbed my attention because the military model has influenced business leadership since the end of World War II, a hierarchical style that served US corporations successfully throughout the second half of the twentieth century.

This style was powerful; it worked.

Deresiewicz, however, sees an urgent need to shift from our lingering bureaucratic model because it selects leaders based on sparkling resumes, which over sixty years has led us to become a land of "world-class hoop jumpers." What's still most important in leadership, Deresiewicz says, are "impressive titles" or "people who can climb the greasy pole of whatever hierarchy they decide to attach themselves to." The danger is that the type of person who climbs that slippery ladder and achieves in this environment is often "commonplace, ordinary, usual" because the skill that moves one up the ladder isn't excellence but "a talent for maneuvering."

Stubbornly, we still admire the twentieth-century technocrat instead of the twenty-first-century original thinker, who needs more freedom and solitude to produce. That's a disaster brewing because technocrats inspire "neither love nor fear nor even respect." What these leaders inspire most is "uneasiness."

Last century's leadership persona was talented at keeping routines going strong but untalented at stimulating a range of people to commit passionately to something that helps others. This leadership style is being pressured to shift because of the Web, especially social media sites such as Facebook, Twitter, YouTube, LinkedIn, and Google+. Rooted in people sincerely connecting with one another, customers not only access information instantly but also learn of vital knowledge to offer others through virtual conversations that quickly can shift to innovation and real-world products and services.

A sharp business model is moving this idea further, the "mesh economy" or sharing-based business that focuses on collaboration. Technology not only helps people connect but also fosters trust between strangers. That's key in a model that focuses on swapping, lending, borrowing, and even sharing skills. Using a strategy known as "collective consumption" (once the norm in rural areas where farmers shared barns and special vehicles), Zipcar is a significantly growing mesh business, a fundamental shift so that people have access to cars that are sprinkled around neighborhoods in dense cities or other populated areas such as universities. By sharing, people in these communities now have access to cars that they once had to buy, maintain, and pay insurance for—even though they rarely used cars since they had access to work and shopping through subways and walking. Zipcar (http://www.zipcar.com) gives them a better option to bypass traditional rental companies when they need a car near their home to drive to a specific location a few times each month without planning or spending a great deal of time going to a rental agency such as Avis or Hertz.

People are more empowered than in the past, and leaders must understand this shift, accept it, and learn how to evolve. In London they've taken the mesh business further through Good Gym (http://www.goodgym.org) with the goal to take an energy surplus to where it's needed. For example, an active jogger can take a three-mile run (which she would do anyway three times each week) with an envelope stuffed with vital information that an elderly man in her neighborhood needs that afternoon. The younger runner uses her exercise time to help an elderly person in her community, a unique connection, a *new herd.*

Hundreds of sharing businesses are arriving, moving away from traditional brick-and-mortars into collective businesses of people that act through trust.

- *Airbub:* books a room in a private home with the owners (or without) all over the world's continents. (https://www.airbnb.com)

- *Kickstarter:* helps people raise money for projects in the arts, including film, art, music, and publishing. (http://www.kickstarter.com)

- *Kiva:* loans twenty-five dollars or more to a farmer or someone in any field in the developing world who needs to create a business; the loans get repaid, without interest. (http://www.kiva.org)

In a 2011 article in *The Atlantic,* Sara Horowitz describes these new businesses as a "Quiet Revolution," or better described as "a return to basics, with a focus on community, health, ecology, happiness, and balance. At its root is the idea of mutualism—people coming together, pooling resources, and meeting their own needs." Even though government and big business are not leading this movement, all leaders should be aware of this growing *new herd* of humans with shared needs who work well together.

Today, however, most businesses are firm (not customer) centric. Leadership must act to increase benefits for the customer as the Web swiftly *moves forward*. Research has predicted that in the next fifty years we'll be dealing with many more people—not simply a pretty unit of measurement cherished in yesterday's businesses. Companies need to embrace customers as the new CEO, or one day they'll be tossed away like rotting fruit.

In his book *The Facebook Effect*, David Kirkpatrick states that the second most visited website after Google is Facebook, a "technological powerhouse with unprecedented influence across modern life." In the viral sense, we have a community that didn't exist before. We're connecting with people from around the globe and from various decades of our lives, another *new-herd* environment that often builds confidence through support and encouragement while guiding us to be aware of ongoing change.

Through social media, people often get validated, the technology encouraging an open (rather than a historic one-way) conversation. This twenty-first-century artificial intelligence is as revolutionary as the telegraph and telephone, and it's causing an uncomfortable change for companies and employees because today anyone around the world can bring information to the table. It's no longer an exclusive club. Last century most of us never had access to information unless we paid money for it. Information was kept secret; most were excluded from obtaining it. Today, however, most of us (not simply the powerful elite) in the US have access, which has resulted in fewer secrets and clubs, while making it easier to communicate, gather information, and act.

After World War II, we relied on corporate conglomerates to advance the economy, launch innovative products, and support our infrastructure. From Sears to IBM, to the big three automakers, all were expected to keep our economy going while being the source of new research and ideas. In essence we allowed corporations to dictate who we were, what we purchased, as well as when and where. But with increasing digital intelligence that connects information and people and things, we're shifting power from the ruling class of corporate giants and restoring power to the people. Leadership that continues to restrict others through *uneasiness* will fail over the next century because the public won't accept that style.

Even though there's significant resistance to the idea that power is truly possessed by the customer, companies such as Amazon, Google, Facebook, and countless other "young" companies (who are not overly capitalized in the traditional sense with brick-and-mortar investments) such as mesh companies are the key source of innovation that will support our open economy.

New Herds—A Stronger Economy Through Education

There are always stealthy *lions of change* out there, crouching in the brush, preparing to attack, and keeping their prey from *moving forward* to feed. Today's *lions of change* are trying to prevent the US educational system from embracing a *new-herd* leadership style.

The documentary *The Finland Phenomenon: Inside the World's Most Surprising School System* reveals why the US has seen a decline in its first-rate K–12 education system. In Finland, the focus is on teachers, not testing and scores. The country developed a system that authentically focuses on people gaining trust with one another instead of the industrial-age focus on metrics and measurements.

Rather than avoiding change, the Fins embraced it by taking an underperforming educational system, renovating it, and creating something fresh—a model that would logically blend with the growing knowledge-based economies in the US. They invested in high-quality teacher preparation, which requires a master's degree, and boosted education as one of the country's most highly esteemed professions, even if it isn't the highest paid. This new approach through preparation echoes Finland's motto "Trust through Professionalism." Teachers are rarely evaluated or disparaged (which reduces *uneasiness*) in Finland's system, which now leads the West as the highest in education quality.

But take a look at the US. In the last twenty-five years, this country's educational reform was led by bureaucratic government and hierarchical business that didn't invite educators into the discussion, the opposite of embracing *new herds* that offer one another vital information. The US used a closed, uneasy, and directive style through which CEOs and government leaders told teachers what they wanted and how to change to produce a better educational system. That top-down leadership style, however, has failed because it was narrowly fixed on the twentieth-century measurement model of "teach to the test," which produced factual recall and memorization, weak skills for our knowledge-based economy that requires an increase in critical and creative thinkers.

Spotting genuine *new-herd* leadership, Harvard Professor Tony Wagner, the documentary's narrator, states that Finland created a better economy through a genuine "bipartisan consensus over thirty years about the importance of education and the importance of high-quality teaching as the real solution. It's been a partnership between businesses, policymakers, and educators, and that's what we need in this country but don't have" ("How Finland Became an Educational Leader" by David Sirota, *Salon*, July 18, 2011).

By blending with *new herds*, Finland adopted better ideas to define excellent teaching and rejected memorization-based curriculum by shifting to twenty-first-century thinking-based curriculum. The economical result of Finland's educational change has led to a global standard of success and excellence. Paralleling the country's educational growth is their economy, which is "rated among the highest in the world in innovation, entrepreneurship, and creativity."

As US educators continue to be denigrated, Finland treats teachers as scientists, and its classrooms as laboratories, in which intellectual preparation continues to develop each decade as teachers work within a strong community—a powerful link to Finland's successful economy. In contrast, education in the US is stuck in nineteenth-century semi-professionalism or, as Wagner describes it, "medieval." Teachers are alone each day, and isolation is the enemy of innovation. The Fins grew by offering teachers time to work together as professionals, to connect and to share ideas, removing them from isolation.

Finland's model contradicts the popular "teacher demonizing" in the US, a reform that still blames teachers for problematic statistics instead of helping them spend more time in broader *herds*, which encourage ongoing professional learning. In the knowledge age, we can no longer treat education as a semi-profession because our economy and its workers won't be able to compete in a tech-flattening world.

Put Yourself in a Different Room

In Margaret Atwood's 1981 short story "Bread," the Canadian author extends the long-term value of connecting through *new herds* when she asks readers to use their imagination by conjuring up a piece of bread. In each paragraph that follows, bread shifts from one challenging environment to another, mirroring how leaders today should strive to use their imaginations so that companies can truly adapt to ongoing change in today's complex global economy.

In the story's opening, the reader doesn't have to imagine bread, because it's in a familiar setting of abundance. Atwood describes bread as ubiquitous, meaningless, or as something "you put butter on...then peanut butter, then honey.... [It] happens to be brown, but there is also white bread, in the refrigerator, and a heel of rye you got last week...now going moldy."

Next "you," the reader, are asked to shift from the carefree developed world where bread is always available and into a barren, challenging environment. By selecting the second-person point of view, Atwood pulls the reader into the story by continually asking *you* to use your imagination, which puts you "into a different room; if you don't use your imagination you stay in the room you're in."

> *Imagine a famine.... You are now lying on a thin mattress in a hot room. The walls are made of dried earth, and your sister... is starving, her belly is bloated, flies land on her eyes.... You are as hungry as she is, but not yet as weak. Should you share the bread or*

give the whole piece to your sister? Should you eat the piece of bread yourself?

In this developing world of extreme poverty, bread now symbolizes a crucial decision of life or death. Bread becomes more than just something that is mindlessly eaten or allowed to rot. The stronger sibling has to decide if she will eat the bread and live, or share it with her weaker, dying sister. A decision must be made.

But there's no answer.

Next Atwood asks *you* to imagine bread being offered to you in prison.

> *There is something you know that you have not yet told. Those in control of the prison know that you know. So do those not in control. If you tell those in charge, thirty or forty or a hundred of your friends, your comrades, will be caught and will die.*

In this setting, bread has become a source of manipulation, temptation, and betrayal. You have a choice to sacrifice your friends in order to save yourself, or to keep quiet and endure nightly hunger and pain.

Again, no answer.

Next Atwood asks you to imagine that the bread leaves the prison so that the loaf weaves into a traditional German fairy tale.

> *There were once two sisters. One was rich and had no children, the other had five children and was a widow, so poor that she no longer had any food left. She went to her sister and asked her for a mouthful of bread. "My children are dying," she said. The rich sister said, "I do not have enough for myself," and drove her away from the door. Then the husband of the rich sister came home and wanted to cut himself a piece of bread; but when he made the first cut, out flowed red blood.*

Everyone knew what that meant.

What everyone knew was that the richer sister made her decision out of selfishness and self-preservation, and the result was clear—*death*. The poorer sister never will have enough for herself.

When you're extremely selfish, your behavior affects others. But when you make decisions that hurt people—like the starving sister with five kids—you don't want to think about it, and that's an ongoing human problem becoming clearer to all of us due to the five-thousand-day-old Web, which triggers an increasingly open, information-sharing, global economy.

Atwood concludes the story by pulling the reader out of three horrendous scenes that include poverty, prison, and a dark German fairy tale. She asks you to imagine the bread back in the developed world of abundance, where it looks different now.

The loaf...floats about a foot above your kitchen table.... There are not strings attaching the cloth to the bread or the bread to the ceiling or the table to the cloth. You've proved it by passing your hand above and below. You didn't touch the bread, though. What stopped you? You don't want to know whether the bread is real or whether it's just a hallucination.

There's a famous quote that says that the role of the artist is to disturb, not to pacify with simple black-and-white answers to life's mysteries. Atwood's role is to ask questions in a unique way, spurring deeper thinking about the world's complexities. She's asking you to see bread as more than it appears to be in the perfect developed world or in an ugly children's fairy tale. By using your *imagination* to "put yourself in a different room," it will be difficult to see bread in a tidy way.

That's a major problem with leadership today. Many don't want to know about these messy, complex settings. Leaders ignore untidiness because in our own world "bread" is easy to deal with and allowed to go moldy. But intuitively, deep down, most of us know that the variety and abundance of bread we eat leads to others "bleeding," especially if we continue to focus only on ourselves rather than *new herds*. With today's Jetson-like technology leading to quick, open access to information, leaders must imagine the world's economy in a "different room" because that's what today's leadership mind must achieve.

In the developed world, bread continues to mirror money. But even if your company is meeting its financial objectives, leadership should *imagine* itself outside of this comforting world and focus on needs where bread (or money) isn't as available—a local community or global customer (such as P&G growing in the developing world by offering inexpensive, much needed products to the world's poor, or Stanford's free online courses for students around the planet).

Atwood's "bread" parallels the call for today's leaders to understand that most of us, including the developed world, will have to deal with some aspect of famine in our lives ahead, whether it's in our educational system, on Main Street and with its workers, or in static corporations and unions and state and federal governments.

If we don't think through these areas of decline (sharing ideas and knowledge to help communities *rise),* we'll end up with only that life-or-death decision of the developing world or prison or German fairy tale. Atwood's conclusion is vital to the call for giraffe-inspired leadership.

> *There's no doubt you can see the bread, you can smell it, it smells like yeast and it looks solid enough, solid as your own arm. But can you trust it? Can you eat it? You don't want to know, imagine that.*

We can't continue that twentieth-century leadership style, an archaic setting in which we *don't want to know,* even in our exploding knowledge age. We must use our *imaginations* to connect with communities that wish to learn. *Giraffes of Technology: The Making of the Twenty-First-Century Leader* is rooted in the metaphor of the tallest herbivore on the planet. The book's themes are not tidy like bread in the developed world or clear like the black-and-white moral in the German fairy tale.

This book's goal is to ask all of us to pay attention to a world in which messy, constant change will be the norm and to keep asking how we can *move forward* together through ongoing learning that helps interact with others around the globe.

My co-author and I researched and wrote *Giraffes of Technology: The Making of the Twenty-First-Century Leader* to spur a *conversation* with you, to attempt to engage all of us to think through twenty-first-century problems, wrestle with them through *imagination* that "puts you in a different room," and to help bread (innovative ideas) shift from the developed to the developing world, and back again—the *new-herd* leadership style.

By using your *imagination*, you trigger the *giraffe's* ability to act as a *lookout post*, spotting dangers and opportunities; to show *empathy* for others, especially those outside your *herd*; to embrace *falls* that lead to a *rise* by continuing to feed through learning; and to be alert for *lions of change* that prevent you from *moving forward* through *new herds*.

Acknowledgments

We have benefited enormously from many people who took time to share their thoughts with us about technology and change, an unusual giraffe metaphor, and America's future. We especially thank Larry Kirshbaum, Bill Cosby, Lisa Leshne, Lisa Hagan, and speeches by Peter Senge and Kevin Kelly.

Many thanks for the cover design suggested by a concept by Andrew W. M. Beierle.

Dr. Glover also thanks his parents Gilbert Jenkins Glover and Minnie Lee Glover for guiding him from a young age to authentically appreciate people.

About the Authors

Dr. Hubert Glover is an experienced CEO and academician who teaches at Drexel University. He has spent more than thirty years leading major enterprises, including subsidiaries of PricewaterhouseCoopers and his own company, REDE, Inc., which has won numerous awards for its services to federal agencies and Fortune 500 companies. He has written more than fifty published articles on corporate governance, auditing, international accounting, and emerging managerial issues. Dr. Glover has gained invaluable experience by working with diverse groups of people in business settings, teaching university students, volunteering for nonprofits, and serving on various boards of directors.

John Curry is an award-winning writer and professor who lectures at the University of Maryland and has taught literature and writing at Santa Monica College and Occidental College. His novella *The Medina Wall* was awarded honorable mention in Paris Belletric's The Archer Prize. He studied with novelist John Rechy, recipient of PEN-USA West's 1997 Lifetime Achievement Award. As secretary of the board at Washington Independent Writers, he co-chaired fiction seminars sponsored by American University, George Mason University, and Johns Hopkins University, events that attracted Pulitzer Prize winner Edward P. Jones, novelist Francine Prose, and others.

* * *

In an effort to spur a *conversation* about *giraffe*-inspired, twenty-first-century leadership, please post any feedback at http://www.giraffesoftechnology.com.

Notes

INTRODUCTION

Bill Cosby's Mark Twain Award Prize history is detailed (along with further reading) at http://www.museum.tv/eotvsection. php?entrycode=cosbybill.

In 1928, Berthold Laufer wrote *The Giraffe in History and Art.* Chapters cover ancient Egypt, China, and India and move through eras of the Middle Ages, the Age of Renaissance, and the nineteenth century (Chicago: Field Museum of Natural History, 1928).

Strong field research (four years observing giraffes in the African wild) reveals the herbivore's inspiring nature. *The Giraffe: Its Biology, Behavior, and Ecology* by Anne Innis Dagg and J. Bristol Foster (Florida: Krieger Publishing Company, 1976).

Jane Stevens writes a unique view of the giraffe (an animal that few scientists have seriously studied) in "Familiar Strangers: What We're Finally Learning about Giraffes" (*International Wildlife.* Jan/Feb. 1993. Volume 23, Issue 1).

"Looking Up" by Jennifer Margulis presents evidence for the survival of the modern giraffe (*Smithsonian:* Nov. 2008, pgs. 37–44).

Chapter One: The Lookout Post—Giraffes of Technology

The chapter opening (in *italics*) by Emily and Ola D'Aulaire was published in "Above the Treetops, They Survey the World," *International Wildlife* (July 1974) 4: 28-31, and it appears in *Tall Blondes: A Book about Giraffes* by journalist Lynn Sherr (Kansas City: Andrews McMeel Publishing, 1997).

To learn more about the twenty-first-century need for "learning organizations," see *The Fifth Discipline: The Art & Practice of The Learning Organization* by MIT's Peter M. Senge (New York: Double Dell Publishing Group, 1990). Two articles about Senge include "Learning for a Change" by Alan M. Webber (Fastcopy.com: Dec. 19, 2007) and "Peter Senge and the Learning Organization" by Mark K. Smith (http://www.infed.org/thinkers/senge.htm).

A late 1990s, cutting-edge book that predicted our confusing future because of digital change, *Blur: The Speed of Change in the Connected Economy* by Stan Davis and Christopher Meyer (Ernst and Young Center for Business Innovation. New York: Warner Books, 1998).

One of the strongest learning organizations (GE) and its leader (Jack Welch) are detailed in *The Jack Welch Lexicon of Leadership* by Jeffrey A. Krames (New York: McGraw-Hill, 2001).

To learn about fresh views of the Digital Age, see "Interlude: A Conversation with Kevin Kelly, Editor of *Wired* Magazine" by Margit Misangyi Watts (Wiley Periodicals, Inc., New Directions for Teaching and Learning, No. 94, Summer 2003) and "Kevin Kelly: The Next 5,000 Days of the Web" (TED: Dec. 2007).

The chapter metaphors and poems include Aesop's fable "The Tortoise and the Hare" (http://en.wikipedia.org/wiki/The_Tortoise_and_the_Hare), the Greek myth of Icarus (http://en.wikipedia.org/wiki/Icarus), and "To a Friend Whose Work Has Come to Triumph," by Anne Sexton, 1962 (http://writersalmanac.publicradio.org/index.php?date=2006/08/20).

Charles Fishman reveals how Walmart's low prices led to global dominance in *The Wal-Mart Effect: How the World's Most Powerful Company Really Works and How It's Transforming the American Economy* (New York: Penguin Books, 2006).

Google culture, which is influencing the twenty-first-century economy, is explored in books such as *The Google Story* by David A. Vise and Mark Malseed (New York: Delta Trade Paperbacks, 2008) and *Googled: The End of the World as We Know It* by Ken Auletta (New York: Penguin Press, 2009).

Warren Buffett's wise investment in freight rail was a key *lookout-post* risk and is a potential long-term success. "Buffett's Not Just Playing with Trains" by Dan Reed (*USA Today*, 3/24/10), and "Warren Buffett Sees Strong Rail System as Key to US Growth" by Dan Reed (*USA Today*, 3/25/10).

Chapter Two: Gentle Giants—Twenty-First Century Communication

The chapter opening (in *italics*) by Ken Stott, Jr., was published in "The Incredible Giraffe," in *Strangest Creatures on Earth* (New York: Sheridan House, 1953), and it appears in *Tall Blondes: A Book about Giraffes* by journalist Lynn Sherr (Kansas City: Andrews McMeel Publishing, 1997).

Two articles about the millennial generation and how this new workforce reacts to archaic leadership styles: "Gen Y and the 2020 Organization" by James Kerr (http://www.management-issues. com/2011/1/17/opinion/gen-y-and-the-2020-organization. asp) and "The Results of Machiavellian Leadership in Today's Times" by Carol Decker (http://www.astd.org/Publications/ Newsletters/ASTD-Links/ASTD-Links-Articles/2012/04/ The-Results-of-Machiavellian-Leadership-in-Todays-Times).

Captain Sully Sullenberger's discusses his leadership style in "Practice Makes Perfect" (*AARP*, Dec. 2009) and *Highest Duty: My*

Search for What Really Matters by Chesley B. Sullenberger and Jeffrey Zaslow (New York: HarperCollins, 2009).

Novartis CEO Dan Vasella's unique corporate leadership is revealed in "What Novartis Sees in Eye Care" by Kerry Capell and Dermot Doherty (*Bloomberg Businessweek*, Jan. 18, 2010) and the *Washington Post's* "On Leadership" interview by Steve Pearlstein with Dan Vasella (http://www.youtube.com/watch?v=OyybubyTMwQ).

To learn more about the Harvard MBA program, see "Harvard Changes Course: School's Curriculum Overhaul Part of a Push to Alter Elite B-School Culture" by Diana Middleton and Joe Light (*The Wall Street Journal*, Feb. 3, 2011).

The shift to the small-business focus on the customer today is explored in "David vs. Goliath" by Jessica Shambora (*Fortune*: Feb. 28, 2011).

This article explores how a major corporation such as P&G takes an anthropological research approach to learn more about the world's poor, our growing customer base: "Can P&G Make Money in Places Where People Earn $2 a Day" by Jennifer Reingold (*Fortune*: Jan. 17, 2011).

Written in the late nineteenth century, "The Open Boat" by Stephen Crane was first published in *Scribner's Magazine* in 1897 and later in the story collection *The Open Boat and Other Tales of Adventure* (New York: Doubleday & McClure Co. 1898). Here's a link where you can read Crane's story: http://public.wsu.edu/~campbelld/crane/open.htm.

Chapter Three: A Violent Birth—The Cycle of Falls and Rises

The chapter opening (in *italics*) appears in *Tall Blondes: A Book about Giraffes* by journalist Lynn Sherr (Kansas City: Andrews McMeel Publishing, 1997).

Technology helped Dr. Elaine Smokewood deal with a health fall while improving her higher education teaching style. "Taught by a Terrible Disease" by Jeffrey R. Young (*The Chronicle of Higher Education/Technology*: Jan. 3, 2010 and the video: http://chronicle.com/article/Taught-by-a-Terrible-Disease/63347).

Actress Lillian Gish dealt with radical twentieth-century change in the silent movie industry. "Don't Wish Upon a Star, Make Yourself One" by Peter Weddle (*HigherEdJobs* blog: July 20, 2010: http://www.higheredjobs.com/blog/postDisplay.cfm?blog=2&post=202&Title=Don%E2%80%99t%20Wish%20Upon%20a%20Star%2C%20Make%20Yourself%20One.

To understand the challenges of success, see "Why Leaders Don't Learn from Success" by Francesca Gino and Gary P. Pisano (*Harvard Business Review*, April 2011).

One of the best dramas of the twentieth century, an American tragedy that focuses on failure and success in business, and in life: *Death of a Salesman* by Arthur Miller (New York: Viking Penguin, 1949).

Chapter Four: Moving Forward—Creating Space for Imagination

The chapter opening (in *italics*) appears in *Tall Blondes: A Book about Giraffes* by journalist Lynn Sherr (Kansas City: Andrews McMeel Publishing, 1997).

For more information on the Luddites' fear of losing jobs and their rejection of change, see "Luddites of the World, Relax!" by Ellen Gibson (*Bloomberg Businessweek* magazine, Sept. 30, 2009).

A wonderful essay about dreaming and how the act often ends after graduating from college: "Daydream Believer" by James Seckington (*The Chronicle Review*, Jan. 22, 2010).

To read more about the award-winning comedic movie *Big*, see http://en.wikipedia.org/wiki/Big.

This book reinforces the idea that as we age dreaming is vital for staying active: *Still Surprised: A Memoir of a Life in Leadership* by Warren Bennis with Patricia Ward Biederman (New York: John Wiley and Sons, Inc., 2010).

Jane McGonigal, a game designer, is considered one of the top thinkers under age thirty-five: "The Game of Life" by Evan R. Goldstein (*The Chronicle Review*, Jan. 14, 2011) and McGonigal's book *Reality Is Broken: Why Games Make Us Better and How They Can Change the World* (London: Penguin Press, 2011).

To learn more about Jeff Bezos and the start of Amazon, see an interview with Jeff Bezos in *A Museum of Living History* (Washington, DC: 2001, Academy of Achievement).

The challenges of hiring less expensive contractors, including the risks and benefits, is explored in "Why America Is Going the Way of the Freelancer" by Tara Moore (CNNMoney, June 22, 2011).

A poem that supports the type of change humans need to achieve in the knowledge age: "Freedom" by William Stafford (1969). Also see the interview with Stafford by Dave Smith of *Modern American Poetry* (February 6, 1971: http://www.english.illinois.edu/maps/poets/s_z/stafford/interview.htm).

Chapter Five: Lions of Change Destroy Creative Settings

The chapter opening (in *italics*) by J. Bristol Foster was published in "Africa's Gentle Giants," in *National Geographic* (Sept. 1977) 402-21, and it appears in *Tall Blondes: A Book about Giraffes* by journalist Lynn Sherr (Kansas City: Andrews McMeel Publishing, 1997).

Mountain climbing, twenty-first-century leadership, and authentic teamwork have a strong connection in the article "A Leadership Nightmare Turned Everest Triumph" by Anne Parmenter (*Washington Post*, April 12, 2010).

Three excellent articles about smart companies engaging in purpose and sustainability to increase company performance: "Duty of Care" by Chrystal Houston (http://maysbusiness.tamu.edu/index.php/duty-of-care); "Why Sustainability is Winning Over CEOs" by Duane Stanford (*Bloomberg Businessweek*, March 31, 2011); and "Snacks for a Fat Planet," by John Seabrook (*New Yorker*, May 16, 2011).

To read more about dialogue and discussion, see "Chapter 12: Team Learning" (pages 233–269) in *The Fifth Discipline: The Art & Practice of The Learning Organization* by MIT's Peter M. Senge (New York: Double Dell Publishing Group, 1990).

Are we having far too many meetings with PowerPoints that don't engage employees? A powerful article that argues for the need to reduce these twentieth-century settings: "Hold Conversations, Not Meetings" by Tony Golsby-Smith (*Harvard Business Review*, HBR Blog Network, Feb. 15, 2011).

To learn more about Maya Angelou's transformative life and her "finishing school," read her autobiography *I Know Why the Caged Bird Sings* (New York: Random House, 1969).

Chapter Six: New Herds—Blending into Diverse Communities

The global shift in higher education via online education is explored in the article "Why Stanford's Free Online Education Experiment Is Booming," by Liz Dwyer (http://www.good.is/post/why-stanford-s-free-online-education-experiment-is-booming/).

A cutting-edge view of marketing in the knowledge age: "Marketing 3.0: Expert Discusses Paradigm Shift and the Now of Marketing" by Chrystal Houston (http://maysbusiness.tamu.edu/index.php/marketing-3-0).

One of the best essays written about this century's leadership, a lecture delivered to the plebe class at United States Military Academy at West Point: "Solitude and Leadership" by William Deresiewicz (*The American Scholar*, March 1, 2010). The speech is also connected to the novella *Heart of Darkness* by Joseph Conrad (first published in 1902).

A *lookout-post* idea that's coming: *The Mesh: Why the Future of Business Is Sharing* by Lisa Gansky (New York: Portfolio Penguin, 2010).

Written by the founder of the Freelancers Union, a nonprofit that represents the growing independent workforce: "Occupy Big Business: The Sharing Economy's Quiet Revolution" by Sara Horowitz (*The Atlantic*, Dec. 6, 2011).

To learn more about twenty-first-century social media, see *The Facebook Effect: The Inside Story of the Company That Is Connecting the World* by David Kirkpatrick (New York: Simon and Schuster, 2010).

Two smart articles that examine the impact of educators, business, and government working together to produce the West's top educational system: "How Finland Became an Educational Leader" by David Sirota (*Salon*: July 18, 2011) and "What Americans Keep Ignoring about Finland's School Success" by Anu Partanen (*The Atlantic*, Dec. 29, 2011).

To read the unique short story "Bread" by Margaret Atwood, visit http://www.qcc.mass.edu/plafountaine/Bread%20MAtwood.pdf.

Made in the USA
Charleston, SC
11 February 2013